In memory of

Kenny
Pete
Kruno
Animal
Skid Row

"I'm always on the lookout for books like this that can make a difference in kids lives. (How To Be A Successful Criminal) not only gives spirit and attitude and philosophy...but also practical...steps to follow to create a life-sustaining career within the law."

Sister Helen Prejean, csj
Author of Dead Man Walking

"As a street cop of 15 years, I was pleasantly surprised after reading Ron's book. It's a must-read for anyone who has lost hope of being part of the American Dream — this book speaks from the heart in the language of the street. I highly recommend it."

Officer Michael Johnson
St. Paul Police Dept.

"I work with kids most of society don't want to know exist. They are all felons. Ron shows them another way. He listens when kids say it's not their fault, they are the way they are — that the world is against them. He doesn't say they're wrong...he tells them to quit taking life laying down...to take some responsibility for their own lives."

Daniel Gill, Corrections Officer
Hennepin County Juvenile Detention Ctr.

"As one of the former leaders of the Black "P." Stone Nation representing Chicago, Milwaukee, Minneapolis and St. Paul, I was at odds with the establishment. I found out the hard way...'there is no free lunch.' Whenever you strike out to 'do your thing,' take the advice of someone who has traveled that route before you. So many of us don't wake up until we hear the gate of the jail cell close behind us."

Sonny Gangster Jackson, Former Leader
Black "P." Stone Nation

"This is a book of urgent importance for everyone — kids and adults, criminals and victims, and anyone who cares about the future."

Mark Chevalier, Lead Counselor
Minneapolis Youth Diversion Program

HOW TO BE A SUCCESSFUL CRIMINAL

The Real Deal on Crime, Drugs, and Easy Money

BY: **RON GLODOSKI**
& ALLEN FAHDEN

WITH: **JUDY GRANT**

Turn Around Publishing
Colorado Springs, Colorado

This book is based upon a series of actual events, but does not constitute a complete accounting of all events. The names and places have been changed to protect the innocent.

Cover design: Mark Herman, Creative Director
Brendan Bathrick, Designer & Illustrator

Book design: Terri Lynn TallTree

Published by
Turn Around Publishing
P.O. Box 7111
Colorado Springs, CO 80933-7111

First Edition

ISBN 0-9666530-0-9

Library of Congress Catalog Number: 98-090654

Printed in the United States of America

Dedicated to

Jay, Todd, Jesse, Megan, Zachary, Jack, and Shay

I want to thank the Creator for allowing me to survive life on the street in order to be of service to anyone who has been told that they're stupid, worthless, or not good enough — those who have been made to feel less than they truly are; for we are all magnificent.

I dedicate this book to all kids everywhere who are living and dying without hope. Never be afraid to dream and work towards a future without violence and fear. You can be anything you want to be.

Table of Contents

PART THREE:
How To Be A Successful Criminal

PART FOUR:
How To Be Successful Without Bein' A
Criminal

Acknowledgments

From The Bottom of My Heart,
A Special Thanks To The Following People
My dear friend, Allen Fahden, for his creative genius. Together we dreamed the original dream for this project.

Judy Grant, and Terri Lynn and Robert TallTree for believing in me and this project enough to contribute blood, sweat, and sometimes tears in order to make this book a reality.

Technical Advisors
Scott Edelstein, Doug Toft, George Cleveland, Catherine Parker, Maria West, Robin Mercier, and Officer Michael Johnson for their guidance and editorial contributions. Mark Herman, Brendan Bathrick, and Marden Petrie for the fabulous job they did on the book cover.

Contributors
Emil Glodoski, Richard Glodoski, Michael Skidmore, William Arner, Sonny Jackson, and Ronny Wagner for the courage they showed by allowing me to use their stories.

Those Who Believed
Leni Erickson, Sherry Goodman, Sheri Sundby, Nell Kaiser, Phil Styrlund, Danny Falk, Gail Anthony, and Roy and Jean Reddemann, for their unwavering encouragement and support.

It is impossible for me to list all the people who, over the past five years, have influenced and encouraged me and the outcome of this book. With my deepest gratitude, I thank you all.

Read This First

Do You Want to Do More Than Just Survive?

This book shows you how to be more than you ever thought you could be.

If you're between the ages of 12 and 22, I *dare* you to read this book! And if you can't read, or don't like to read, then find somebody else to read it and fill you in on what you missed.

If you've ever felt isolated, ignorant, or not good enough, *read this book.*

Do you want to learn how to survive out on the streets? *Then use this book.* Do you want to learn how to do more than just survive? *Then use this book.* If you know you're one bad mother but don't know what you got to lose — *read this book.*

If you're tired of being out on the street, and wonder what you should do next, *read this book.* If you're a wanna-be — *read this book.*

This book's about crime. It's about choices. It's about attitude. It's about survival.

It's not meant to be everything you ever wanted to know about crime and success. It's information I've put together that will help you do more than survive — if you dare to use it.

A word to you ladies: As you read this book, you're gonna notice I talk to the brothers. But, just so you know, I didn't do this to exclude or disrespect you. I know there's a whole lot of you sisters out there who need the information in this book, and I'm talkin' to you as much as I'm talkin' to them.

Ron

To Parents And Professionals Who Pick Up This Book

Read this book at your own risk!

I guarantee that you will find something in these pages which will insult your morality, and challenge your sense of what is proper. Just know that my writing style is not meant to sensationalize or shock — it is meant to maximize communication with kids. Please don't close your mind before your heart has an opportunity to experience the true message.

Crime, violence, and death have become commonplace to the kids of America. Between 1983 and 1992, the arrest of adults for violent crimes increased by 21%, while juvenile arrests increased 117%. Juvenile murder arrests rose 128%, aggravated assault arrests rose 95%, and juvenile arrests for other assaults increased 106%.

Now I don't know what that says to you, but it tells me that we are raising a generation of frightened, neglected high-risk kids who are isolated, depressed, and out of control. These kids are in crisis, and are crying out for help. They have turned to drugs, crime, and violence to numb their pain and provide them with a sense of value and identity.

When you're young, crime can look like a short cut to the good life: money, power, sex, and prestige. It's easy to get caught up in the deadly game being played out across our country today.

Criminal gangs are no longer just a big city thing. There's hardly a town that doesn't have a problem with juvenile crime and violence. What the hippie culture was to the kids of the sixties, the subculture of the gangster gang is to the kids of the nineties.

Federal studies indicate that if trends in violence continue as they have over the past 10 years, juvenile arrests for violent crime will at least double by the year 2010. Unless we have the courage to stand beside our kids, and support them as they fight for their lives, we will continue to lose them.

I am not a psychiatrist, psychologist, social worker, or professional educator. I am a 46 year old businessman who survived an abusive childhood by creating a reputation for being a danger to society. By the time I was 15, I had a felony record consisting of armed robbery, strong-armed robbery, assault and battery, and car theft. For ten years I ran one of the largest drug networks in Milwaukee.

At age 34 I was tired of the gangster life I was leading. I had lost my family, and most of my friends were either dead or doing time. I wanted out. But I knew that I would never be able to do it on my own. I needed help.

It started on a dare. Help came from a very unlikely place: a group of super-straight professional men who belonged to the men's group I attended. These men became my new best friends. They encouraged me and cheered for me. They dared me to see myself through new eyes.

I escaped death and imprisonment to learn that I did not have to remain a victim of my past or present circumstances. I discovered that my only real limitations are those I place upon myself.

It is my intention for this book to be a message of hope for kids today.

I invite kids who read this book to dare to believe that they have options other than dying or doing time — and to have the courage to reach out for help expressing their personal power in positive, life-sustaining ways. It is meant to be a small personal contribution toward solving some very frightening, complex problems.

If you don't like what I've done, or how I've done it — good. Then maybe you'll get off your butt and come up with something better. This is not a time for cowardice, ambivalence, or inaction. If we are to reach even a few, it will take a concerted effort of the many.

Ronald J. Glodoski
St. Paul, Minnesota
September 1998

PART ONE:

Most Criminals Suck at Crime

CHAPTER 1

What Do Ya Got To Lose?

Most Criminals Suck At Crime
That's right brother, you heard me. I said, most criminals suck at crime.

So, listen and listen good, 'cuz I'm only gonna say this once. I bet you think you're somethin' just because you pulled a job or two, or sold a couple dime bags of dope. Well, that ain't nothin'! Most suckers I know started out just like you. You hate authority, and you hate the system. You feel there's no place in it for you, so you start tryin' to rip it off. Then you succeed at pullin' one or two jobs and begin to think you're really gettin' over.

But, are you?

Who Am I To Be In Your Face?
I'm someone who's smarter than you're gonna be if you don't read this book.

By the time I was 12, I was runnin' with one of the biggest street gangs in Milwaukee. My juvenile arrest record was a mile long.

At age 15, I was a convicted felon. I'd been arrested for armed robbery, strong-armed robbery, car theft, and assault and battery. When I was in my twenties I rode with members of the motorcycle gangs, the Heaven's Devils and the Milwaukee Outlaws.

At times between 1975 and 1985, I was one of the biggest dope dealers in Milwaukee. It's funny to me now, but back then I actually thought that I was one of the *baddest dudes* in town.

The truth is, I wasn't meaner, tougher or badder than anyone else, I just worked smarter. I developed my own rules for success and worked my business by these rules — until I got so strung out on coke that I forgot to follow them.

I flipped dope for a livin' while I used a day job at a Milwaukee brewery as a cover. I went from dealin' pot to dealin' coke, and made more money in one day than you can even imagine. I had a house, cars, guns, bodyguards, and coke groupies. And for a whole lotta years the law hardly touched me. It wasn't unusual for me to carry around $100,000 in cash. I lived the kind of life you dream of, but will probably never have — not because you're not mean or tough, or smart enough, but because you're so deep into your own stuff that you don't see how things really are, and before you know it, you'll blow it.

America's Dumbest Criminals

How do I know? Because sooner or later, almost everybody blows it. The question is *when,* not *if.* You're probably tellin' yourself that you're smarter than that. Yeah, every con sittin' in the joint swears that he's smarter than that. But guess what, they're still sittin' there doin' time.

The thing is, you probably won't mess up in the exact same way the guys do who get their story told on America's Dumbest Criminals. But there are different categories of stupid, and eventually you'll get caught up in one of them. You'll either be too high, too scared, too sloppy, too greedy, too confident or too mad.

Let's say you and one of your boys get high and decide to hit a convenience store. The thing is, you don't know that the guy's been hit before and now he's got the most heavily armed store in the neighborhood. You just walked into your worst nightmare: no money in the till and a vigilante store owner pointin' a gun at your chest. What are you gonna do? Order a Slurpee or blow him away?

Now because you're so messed up, you panic and you try to take him out. The trouble is, he's scared and ragin' mad, but he's not high, so he's thinkin' clearer, and has better reflexes than you. Where does that leave you? On the floor in a pool of your own blood, or in the back of a squad car on the way to the slammer. Or just maybe you and your friends wind up killin' the poor guy, so now you've got a murder rap to look forward to. And all of this for the measly seven bucks in the till.

Alright, alright, just for argument's sake, let's say you pulled a job, and you didn't blow it. You beat the odds. You didn't get blown away, and you walked away with some cash. Do you know how to keep from screwin' it up afterwards?

Wake Up, Brother

Look, I know you're not stupid. It's just that you probably don't organize or plan. You go through life asleep — never really thinkin' about what you're doin'. But, man, if you want to play in this game, you gotta wake up and think!

The truth is, most of us get busted or go back to the same old place we've always lived, and keep on havin' nothin'. Why? Because you blow the money on dope before you ever get home, or you throw it away gamblin', or partyin' with some woman.

Or maybe you're like I was when I was younger, and you just don't care. My juvenile record is a mile long because I didn't care about myself, or anybody else. I wanted to get caught. It was better in the joint than it was at home. Jail was a picnic to me. Probably 50% of my friends were in the joint.

So, if you're like I was, and want to get caught, fine — go ahead: mess up and get busted. And if you wanna do somethin' really thoughtless, get yourself a couple of life sentences. You'll *never* have to worry about home again. The thing is, there'll probably come a time when you've had enough of the joint. Then what?

"Get a Life" Doesn't Mean a Life Sentence
Most suckers go through life asleep. They stumble along and get caught up in the nightmare they call their lives, until one day they wake up in the joint, or paralyzed from the neck down, or dead.

A few months ago, a guy I know was given two consecutive life sentences *without parole* for his alleged involvement in two execution-style killings. He's 23 years old and has never been in serious trouble with the law before, but he'll spend the rest of his life in prison because he allowed himself to become part of a situation that got out of control.

He and the guys he was with got caught up in the heat of the moment and all of them lost their lives: two from gunshot wounds, the rest from bein' there when it happened. He wasn't the shooter, he was just a punk. A punk that went along. Common sense should've told him this wasn't a good deal.

He didn't even know all the guys he was with. He believed that they were just gonna scare some dudes and leave. The next thing *he* knows, some crazy sucker pulls the trigger, and now they're all payin' for the rest of their lives.

It Wasn't Supposed To Happen This Way

This situation went from simple intimidation to the point where some hothead, lookin' for a reputation, decided to blow the suckers away.

The deal is, my friend didn't really have his own game plan — a strategy that would've increased his chances of stayin' in control of his life. He just went with the flow and got caught up in the heat of the moment. He didn't think about what might happen. He didn't bother to check out who he was dealin' with. He didn't know the shooter well enough to know there was a good chance that the fool would go off like that.

So my friend sat on the witness stand sayin', "It wasn't supposed to happen this way!" But the court held him just as responsible for the killings as it did the shooter, and now he'll never see the light of day.

Look At What You've Got To Lose

How'd you like to be your state's youngest adult? It might interest you to know that the Feds have passed a law that allows 13-year-olds to be prosecuted as adults if they commit violent crimes like murder, armed robbery, or rape. You can't hide behind your age anymore. If you don't think about what could happen, man, you're an idiot.

If you're willin' to pay the price for your actions, go for it! You've heard the old sayings, "If you wanna play, you gotta pay" and "If you can't do the time, don't do the crime." The bottom line: make sure you know what you're riskin'.

Makin' Choices

You're not cool when you're dead. You're cold.

Anytime you confront two other kids and they're gang members, know they might be packin'. Now you face the question of whether it's worth shootin' somebody, or possibly gettin' shot. Think about it, man! Is this worth losin' your life over? Is it worth the time you'll be spendin' on death row, and the dead man's walk before they fry you?

Nothin' or nobody on the streets is worth your life! And don't tell me that you were disrespected, or give me that crap about rep. Nobody's gonna care about how bad you were after you're dead. All they'll remember is that you're *dead*.

Where I Drew The Line
I'm not proud of it, but there were times I had to decide whether or not I would blow someone away. I had a lot to protect: my family, my money, my reputation. If someone messed with me, I was definitely gonna keep the fool from doin' it again.

I'd never kill anybody over money, or property, or a woman. I'd hurt somebody. I'd put somebody in the hospital. But as long as they didn't take out one of my family, I wouldn't take their life. I'm grateful that I can say I never killed anybody.

When I was on the street there weren't as many killin's. But today, too many people just don't value life — their own, or anybody else's. There are lots of people, including kids, who will take somebody out for next to nothin'. Some gangs even make murder part of their initiation process.

So check out the people you get involved with. Know who they are, and whether they can stay cool under pressure. If you don't know whether you can count on all of them, blow off the deal.

Wake up! If you don't have a winnin' game plan for your own life, you're gonna end up losin' by some other guy's rules. It's your choice.

Think About It

- *Only 5% of the players are makin' 90% of the real money.*
- *There's a whole lot of stupid people out there. Choose not to be one of them.*
- *"Get a life" doesn't mean a life sentence.*
- *Wake up before you get caught up in some other guy's nightmare. Choose your partners very carefully!*

CHAPTER 2

What Do You Call A Stupid Criminal? INMATE

You probably think the really cool guys are the ones you meet in jail. They've been around. They really know the score, especially the old timers. Everyone in the joint looks up to them. You listen to *these* guys and you can't go wrong — right?

It's No Accident That "Jail" Rhymes With "Fail"

Why do you think these guys are locked up? If they did it right, they'd be where you think you want to be. Nice crib, big car, cash, blow, and women.

But where are they? They're walkin' the line with all the other guys who wound up in the joint. You really think somebody's big time when they eat off the same metal plate that all the other stiffs do?

Let's get it straight. Old timers are expert at survivin' in the joint — not on the street. Of course, there are always exceptions. There are those few guys who've run million dollar businesses from their prison cell, but the odds are, you ain't that guy.

How To Be Your Own Worst Enemy

When you brag about how big you are or the size of the ship-ment you're expecting, you're advertisin' to cops, snitches and other bad dudes who'll hit you. This is one of the worst things you can do.

Now, most likely you're in the business because you think that crime is cool or because deep down you think you can't do anything else.

So you're tryin' to prove that you're as good as, if not better than, everybody else. Guess what? The more you try to prove you're not a punk, the more you become one.

If all you want is for people to think you're bad, go ahead, advertise. Tell every snitch on the block your business! But if you really want to take care of business, stop actin' like you're a reporter for *People Magazine*. When you pull a job, keep your mouth shut. Even though you're tryin' to get people to think you're cool, the smart guys will know you're an idiot, because they already know what you're learnin' for the first time. They've paid their dues, but you're still standin' in the collection line.

To Stay On The Outside, Cover Your Backside

If you want to make it, find somebody who has successfully spent his or her adult life on the streets to become your mentor or teacher.

One of the first things they'll tell you is that you need a good lawyer. 'Cuz if you don't have the right lawyer when you need one, you can kiss your butt goodbye.

In a business where the average person lasts two to three years, I was lucky enough to last ten. I did a lot of bad things, but after I was 17 years old, I never did any hard time. Sure, I got busted a couple of times, but within a day or two my lawyers would have me off on a *technicality.* Big word, technicality.

This means that maybe there's a way to get around the law — even if you're guilty.

The deal is, most court-appointed attorneys ain't worth the paper their diplomas are printed on. If you wanna walk, you have to be willin' and able to shop for your own representation. You have to hire your own lawyer. Someone who works for *you,* not the court system. And you have to be able to pay him enough to keep his attention and motivate him to work. If you don't have a good lawyer, the cops will be more likely to mess with you any way they can.

When Someone Rips You Off, You Can't Call 911
In the 1980's, my oldest brother worked a construction day job in Texas. On weekends he'd fly home to Milwaukee, and fly back to Texas with 50 pounds of pot. By Tuesday or Wednesday it'd all be gone. He was makin' three grand a week just sellin' pot.

He had a sweet thing goin' until one of the locals broke into the glove compartment of his car and stole $7,000. Richie called the police. This was not one of his better moves. When they came to check out his car, they found a lot of pot seeds on the floor, and became curious about him. My brother got mad and decided to put a contract on the kid who ripped him off. But somehow the kid found out about it and got so scared he ratted on Richie.

The Power Of a Technicality
To make a long story short, the cops raided Richie's house on a Wednesday, and only found his personal stash. By this time everything else had been sold. Well, this really ticked them off! So when the cops discovered his coke scale and Dehring grinder with seven milligrams of residue on them, they decided to charge him with the cocaine, too. Fortunately, his lawyer was able to get the charge dropped.

When the cops saw that their case against Richie was goin' down the drain, they decided to manipulate the evidence by adding a bag of seeds to the two ounces of pot they had found. You see, at that time in Texas, any weight over a quarter pound would allow them to charge Richie with a felony. It almost worked, but his lawyer pointed out that seeds and stems don't have THC content. Because of this technicality, Richie ended up with a misdemeanor, and paid a $1,000 fine to the court and $10,000 to his lawyer.

A Lesson I Learned The Hard Way
I always kept $30,000-40,000 set aside for a good lawyer. There was only one time I broke my own rule, and as a result, I ended up gettin' stuck with probation. I had loaned my Trans Am to one of my suppliers who had come in from Toledo. He got wasted and the cops ended up bringin' him back to my house.

It was December and I'd decorated a seven foot marijuana tree with lights and Christmas ornaments. When the cops saw it, they decided to get a warrant and arrest me for possession of marijuana. They came and took my Christmas tree as evidence — lights, ornaments, and all.

I thought it was just a laughable case. I didn't want to spend the money for a lawyer, so I represented myself. Boy, was I surprised when the judge gave me two years probation. It really ticked me off. I learned an important lesson the hard way. *Always buy the services of a good lawyer.*

You know I'm tellin' you the truth. Just look at O.J. Simpson's case. I'm not makin' a judgement here — only a simple observation — 'cuz you and I both know that it never mattered one way or the other whether he was guilty or innocent. He'd been tried and convicted in the media, and in the eyes of most of the world he'll always be guilty. But he had the money to put together a legal dream team. As a result, he beat the odds and walked away a free man.

Hangin' With Fools

The problem with bein' good at crime is that some of your friends are probably fools.

Here's what I mean: When I was 15, I was sent to jail for armed robbery, strong-armed robbery, assault and battery, and auto theft. While I was in the joint, I hooked up with a guy named Chester who was very charismatic and powerful. He had the respect of all the guys in the joint. To be a close associate of Chester's was a very big deal.

Choosin' Stupid Friends Is Like Bein' Stupid Yourself

Chester was really good at breakin' and enterin', so when we got out of the joint we did some jobs together. I figured I could learn somethin' from him; and I did! I learned that he was a freakin' maniac who liked to do more than rip people off. The first thing he did when he broke into a place was case the cupboards and freezer in order to figure out what kind of meal he was gonna make for himself.

That's right, I said meal! This crazy sucker would cook himself a big meal and sit in front of the TV and eat it. I'd be busy workin' the house, and Chester would be fixin' himself a T-bone steak and eggs. Of course he never cleaned up after himself. I'm tellin' you, the guy drove me crazy. I was used to a clean in and out in five minutes or less. But this punk always had to play house! It was all part of his game. He wanted to violate the homeowner, not just make some quick cash. It didn't take me long to tell him he was on his own. A few years later I heard that a homeowner walked in on him and blew him away.

The point is: just because your home boy is willin' to risk his own game doesn't mean you have to play by his rules. Go by your own rules, and always stack the odds in your own favor. It's not just *how* you play, but *how long* you're around to play that makes the difference.

There's Only One Thing Worse Than A Stupid Friend — A Lyin', Cheatin', Rattin' Friend

When I came up, the first rule I learned was *never, ever* snitch. No matter what, you never rat on somebody. It was a rule I lived my life by. Loyalty and honor were very important, and I had a small group of brothers I knew I could always rely on, and who knew they could always rely on me. I would have died for these guys, and they would have died for me. I knew that when I trusted them with $50,000-100,000 cash, they would still have it one day or one year later.

Over the last twenty years many of the new people comin' up don't honor this code. If you happen to be one of these people, I think it's only fair to let you know what can happen to a snitch. Then you'll able to make a smart choice about how to cover your own back.

It Doesn't Take Much To Turn a Mule Into a Rat

In the 80's, JR, a friend of mine who was livin' with my brother Richie, was sent to Jamaica to pick up a couple kilos of coke and hash oil. It turned out that the whole operation was really a sting, set up by the DEA. JR only made it back as far as Chicago, where he was picked up at O'Hare International Airport with all the stuff. It was obvious that somebody in Milwaukee had set him up because the Feds knew exactly when he had left Milwaukee, what airline he had taken, and what time he was arrivin' back at O'Hare.

Well, this up-standin' friend of ours ended up rattin' out quite a few brothers in Milwaukee. And when he agreed to testify in court it made some big people very nervous.

The Contract

Word quickly got out on the street about what was goin' on and a contract was put on JR. People knew that he was livin' with Richie, so, out of respect for me, I was called and told about the decision. I said that they couldn't hit JR because they might get Richie. They told me they didn't care, and to tell my brother to move, because "if he gets in the way, he's goin' down, too."

There was no way I could let my brother get taken out for this snitch, so I told the guy that I was gonna let Richie and JR know what was comin'. I knew Richie, and there was no way he'd back down from a threat like this, no matter what, so I tried to talk them out of hittin' JR. I was finally told that they would give JR a week to get out of town. "If he disappears, there's no reason to go after him, but if he stays to testify we're gonna get him."

I let JR and Richie know what I'd heard. They just laughed and said, "Let 'em come, let 'em come. We can handle 'em." These two were so strung out that they thought they were invincible. It really ticked me off that Richie would ignore the warnin' and put us all in jeopardy because of this snitch!

The Hit

One week later, outside the house he shared with my brother, JR was shot in the face five times. His head was blown apart like a melon, and he died before he ever hit the ground. At the time, Richie was at home and there was some coke, Quaaludes, $10,000, and 30 pounds of my pot in the house.

Richie heard the shots and thought that they were gonna come in for him. He didn't know what was goin' down, but he knew that whatever it was, it sure wasn't good. He had to leave all my pot. All he could do was grab the money and coke and run out the back door.

From the bar down the street he called a friend, who took him to our safe dope house. I learned later that his friend eventually took him over to his girlfriend's house, where he spent the night.

Who Shot JR?

When the cops arrived, they found parts of JR's head and body on the sidewalk three doors from Richie's house. The rest of his head was lyin' in the street. They went into the house, where they discovered my 30 pounds of pot, a couple of guns, and some paraphernalia. Of course, when they couldn't find Richie, they figured that he had killed JR.

At 7 a.m. the next mornin', I got the shock of my life when the cops showed up and presented me with a warrant to search for Richie. Here I was, happy-go-lucky Ronnie, goin' out my door to work, findin' my house surrounded by cops. They asked me where Richie was, and I told them that I had no idea — which I didn't. Truthfully, the only thing on my mind was the two pounds of cocaine I had downstairs sittin' on my scale.

By this time I had begun to get really lazy. I'd been in business about six years and I'd gotten sloppy and had begun to lose my edge. All I could think was, "Oh, my God, they're gonna find my stash." I knew I could beat the rap because they hadn't come with a warrant lookin' for dope, but I would still end up losin' about $100,000.

Richie Calls In The Nick Of Time

You won't believe what happened next! Just as the cops began their search, the phone rang. It was Richie. He was callin' to let me know what had happened. The phone rang at the exact right moment.

Boy, was I ticked. I handed the phone over to the cops, and Richie told them that he and his lawyer would meet them downtown and he'd turn himself in. The cops left without ever searchin' my house.

Richie Charged With Murder

Richie was charged with murder and his bail was set at $50,000. He called and asked me to pay it for him. I told him to forget it because I was so mad at him for gettin' in the situation in the first place. I'd warned him, but he was so messed up on drugs he wouldn't listen. Besides, I'd already lost a bundle on this deal because of the marijuana, and I figured I'd never see the $50,000.

Murder charges were dropped against Richie when an eyewitness picked somebody else out of the lineup. However, they charged Richie with possession of narcotics and guns. This time when he called me to post his bail, I brought the $7,000 in a brown paper sack ($5's, $10's and $20's) and dumped it on the desk at the court house. This was *not* the smartest thing I've ever done.

JR Didn't Need Enemies — His Friends Set Him Up

JR never knew what hit him. We later found out that his friend had set him up. The guy had stopped by the house and told JR that he had run out of gas, and needed some help gettin' his car out of the middle of the street. Richie offered to go down and help them, but the guy told him that he and JR could take care of it.

They walked out of the house and JR never knew what hit him. We never did know who did the hit — whether it was the friend, or somebody waitin' outside.

Later JR's friend claimed he had been forced to do it by the people who ordered the hit. He said that they threatened to kill him and his family if he didn't go along with the plan. Who knows if he was tellin' the truth? Like I said, we never really knew what actually happened.

The Grand Jury

Now this turned into a very bad scene because the hit took

place two blocks from the home of the Chief of Police. It was a major embarrassment, and you'd better believe that the citizens of Milwaukee wanted a full investigation into the matter.

A grand jury was called, and for the next few weeks, it was probably colder in hell then it was on the streets of Milwaukee. The heat was on and I was subpoenaed to testify. Testifyin' before the grand jury was one of the most stressful things I've ever faced, to say nothin' of what it cost me in legal fees. In all, I ended up losin' $25,000 — $15,000 for the pot and $10,000 on lawyers.

Protect Yourself From Snitches
Trust only the people you know. And don't even trust them.

Snitches come in all colors, sizes, and shapes. When you're out on the street playin' the game, you have to cover your own back because there ain't anybody else out there who's gonna do it for you. They're all too busy lookin' out for themselves. Most of them are very willin' to give you up, if they think it'll save their own butt. *Just remember, there are a lot of guys in the joint who were sure that their friends weren't snitches.*

Ninety-five percent of drug-related arrests are made with the help of snitches. There's no 100% protection, especially if you're flippin' dope. But there are some rules that I lived by that kept me in the game a lot longer than most guys. Some of 'em I learned the hard way; some I learned by watchin' other people.

Don't Do Business With a Junkie
I learned this lesson from a close friend of mine named Billy. He and one of his partners ended up doin' a little over a year in LA County jail because they tried to do some serious business with a guy who rolled over on them because he was a junkie.

The Sting
Billy's partner, Pete, knew a guy in California who claimed he

had a contact interested in scorin' 10 to 15 kilos of cocaine a month if the deal was right. Pete asked Billy to go with him and meet the buyers, so he picked up a couple of kilos and they headed for LA.

Everything went great, and the guys in LA said they wanted thirty more kilos. The buyers looked like real high rollers. They owned a chain of Mexican restaurants, drove a new Mercedes and owned a huge house on the beach. They told Billy and Pete they had to leave town for a few days, but insisted that my buddies stay and play at the beach house and use the 'Vette and Porsche while they were gone.

So Billy called and arranged to have the stuff brought out to LA. The old guy from Detroit who was Billy's main connection for this deal got excited about the potential quantities bein' discussed. He decided he should check things out for himself. A few days later he arrived in LA with five kilos wrapped like a birthday present.

Busted
The high rollers got back and arrangements were made for the transaction to be complete. The switch was made. Everything seemed to go down just fine until Billy and Pete got about five miles down the road and were picked up by the California Bureau of Investigation (CBI) and the DEA.

After five days in jail, the cops moved Billy's Detroit buddy into the cell with him. Billy took one look at the guy and saw that he was in bad shape. This was an older pizza-connection guy who always wore expensive three-piece pinstripe suits, and here he was — beat up, filthy, and ragged. He'd lost his glasses, so at first he didn't realize who he was with. When he finally recognized Billy he said, "I'm gonna have to have you killed, Billy. I don't want to, but I have to."

He saw Billy was eatin' breakfast and asked him if he was gonna eat his eggs. Billy said, "No, here," and gave his breakfast to him. The old man looked over at Billy and said, "Thanks, but I'm still gonna have to kill ya." Billy knew he was serious.

Pete Takes The Rap

It turned out that Pete's connection was strung out on heroin and had gotten busted with the real owner of the beach house, restaurant and cars. As soon as he started jonesin' he went bad, and began snitchin'. As a result, my buddies got caught up in a huge DEA sting. The "buyers" were actually undercover agents of the DEA and the CBI.

Fortunately, Pete was a stand-up guy. He took the rap and did the hard time for Billy and the old man. Billy and his buddy from Detroit did just a little over a year on drastically reduced charges and nothin' was ever said again about havin' Billy killed.

Followin' My Own Rules Saved My Butt

There is one incident I'll never forget. My brother Richie checked himself into a Rehab Center for thirty days, and while he was there, he met a guy named Nelson who had some dynamite coke connections. Richie kept tellin' me that I needed to hook up with this guy, so I set up a meeting with him. Richie was right. This stuff was some of the purest coke I ever tasted, so we started doin' a little business.

Nelson Tries To Set Me Up

After a few months, one of my guys tells me that he heard that Nelson had gotten busted. I called my brother to check out the story, but Richie said he hadn't heard anything. I decided to check it out for myself, so I went to see the guy.

Now Nelson owned a successful liquor store in the inner city, and I was one of the few white customers he had. As soon as I got down there, I noticed two white detectives parked across the street from his store. They stuck out like neon lights at night. I couldn't believe it.

So I went in the store and said, "Hey, Nelson, what's happenin'?" and he told me that he had two kilos for me. Now there was no way I was gonna walk out of that store holdin' two kilos of his coke, with the detectives waitin' for me outside. So I told him to give me a sample and I'd check it out and get back to him the next day. He wasn't happy about it and kept tryin' to get me to take it all. Finally he gave me what I asked for and I split.

Avoidin' The Trap
The next day I went back to Nelson's. When I walked in the door, I noticed two white undercover cops trying to blend in with the customers. Now I knew for sure that he was hot!

I told him that his stuff was crap and that I didn't want it. Well, he began to get all crazy on me. He started whinin' at me that I knew his stuff was pure and that I'd better take it and get rid of it for him. I told him to go screw himself, that I wasn't in business anymore, and I walked out of the store.

That was the last time I saw Nelson. He called me repeatedly, but I kept tellin' him no. I later heard that he had set up a lot of other suckers. If I'd gotten greedy, and ignored what my gut was tellin' me, I'd be tellin' this story from the joint.

Hard Choices vs. Hard Time
Now, I've lived long enough to learn that I'm not responsible for the choices somebody else makes for themselves. I'm only responsible for the choices that I make. So listen good: this is not about judgin'; it's about choices.

When you're the one sittin' in that little room with the detectives, it's your butt that's on the line, not anybody else's. If you feel you have to snitch, just know what the consequences could be.

Remember this: The cops are not your friends. At least, most of them aren't. They're not your friends, and they don't want to be your friends. What they want is to do their job. Their job is to keep your neighborhood and everybody else's neighborhood safe. Don't ever doubt that they'll use every means at their disposal to keep the streets safe.

Now if you're out there playin' gangster, flippin' dope, or generally disruptin' your neighborhood, chances are you're gonna get busted. So eventually you'll be given a chance to help them by rattin' out one of your brothers.

Just remember that the cops make recommendations to the DA, and the DA makes recommendations to the judge. In about 99 percent of the cases the DA and judge will go along with the recommendations of the cops. Especially if the case couldn't have been solved without the help of the snitch.

The Cops' Greatest Weapon Against Crime Is a Snitch

If you agree to testify against one of your friends, you're likely to be labeled for life. You might as well pack up and move on, because life as you know it just came to an end. Snitchin' is a high stakes game you play with your life. If you're one of the lucky ones, you'll live to start over somewhere else. If not, you'll probably become just a dusty old photo on your grandmother's bookshelf.

Your Best Friend Will Give You Up
To Save His Own Butt

Maybe you just sold your buddy a quarter ounce of blow and the cops pick him up before he can dump the stuff. They've been watchin' him because they already busted one of the punks he's been flippin' to and that punk ratted on him.

Now the cops are tellin' him that if he doesn't give you up he's gonna spend the next ten years or more in the joint. They tell him that if they had you instead of him, you'd drop a dime on him in a minute! And they'd probably be right because the cops are professionals who are committed to gettin' people to talk in order to protect society from criminals like you. *Cops play all the angles, and most people crumble under the pressure.*

They'll lie to you, threaten you, bully you. If you're young, they'll scare you by tellin' you that you'll end up somebody's girl in the joint. And the thing is, you know they're right. They'll run the good cop/bad cop game on you. They'll pretend to be concerned about you, your kids, your momma, and your grandmomma. They know how to mess with your mind. They've made a science of it. When you get caught you'll be faced with the most difficult decision you've ever had to make in your life: snitch or do the time.

Think About It

- *Don't become your own worst enemy. Keep your mouth shut unless you want every snitch on the block to know your business.*
- *You can't trust anybody. Just remember that there are a lot of guys sittin' in the joint who were sure their best friends weren't snitches.*

PART TWO:

Growin' Up
On The
Street

How To Be A Successful Criminal
The Real Deal On Crime, Drugs, and Easy Money

CHAPTER 3

My Early Years —
Were They Like Yours?

Why Would You Wanna Listen To Me?
Where've I been and what do I know?

I usually don't talk about what it was like growin' up in my house. It's just not somethin' I think about anymore. But I'll tell you about it, so you can know that someone who starts out like you can make it. *You don't have to keep bein' victimized by poverty, violence, loneliness, or pain.*

I don't think my childhood was very different than a lot of other people's. Let's face it, no matter who you are or how great your parents are, bein' a kid's not easy.

Most people experience some kinda fear and pain growin' up. Maybe not the emotional terror and physical violence my brothers and I lived with; it doesn't matter, it all hurts the same. There are parents who'd never physically hurt their kids, but they verbally abuse them every day. Other kids have parents who are almost never around, and that's also very painful.

Everybody has a story — especially today. I don't know your

story, but I know you've got one. This is mine.

To The Outside World We Were Just An Average Middle-Class Family
We were the Cleaver family, all right. But less like "Leave It To Beaver" and more like a meat cleaver.

As a kid, I didn't know my family was different from anybody else's. I really didn't think about it much. I was too busy strugglin' to survive.

I grew up in a middle-class neighborhood on the north side of Milwaukee. There were four of us kids. Richie was the oldest, Emil was two years younger than him, I'm two years younger than Emil, and Kenny was about two years younger than me.

Just before I entered kindergarten, my parents bought the two-family home we shared with my mother's parents. When I was nine, my grandmother had a stroke and became an invalid. She died when I was 11. My grandfather was a very bright man with a gentle soul. He was more of a father to us than our dad ever was. He was the only real father I ever knew. He cared about us boys and we knew it. We loved him.

My Old Man
My dad grew up in a suburb of Milwaukee called West Allis. He was one of five kids from a hardworkin' second generation Polish family. He was a tool and die man, and his dad was a tool and die man.

My old man wasn't very close to his family, and when he was 17 he left home to join the Navy. It was the Second World War, and recruiters weren't checkin' an eligible recruit's age too closely.

After the war he tried to go back to school and get his diploma. But he was 20 years old, and after everything he'd been through, it was just too hard for him to relate to high school. Instead, he took a tool and die apprenticeship and began workin' at Kearney and Trecker, the company his dad worked for.

Everybody Loved My Dad
Except The People Who Should Have

Other people would describe my old man as a wonderful, fun lovin' friend — a good guy with a big heart who'd give his friends the shirt off his back. Most of his life he worked two jobs: full time at the tool and die company and part time for a truckin' firm. His truckin' buddies were his drinkin' and partyin' buddies. He had lots of friends, and fortunately for us, he spent most of his time with them or one of his girlfriends.

At home, life with my dad was a nightmare we couldn't escape by just wakin' up. He bullied and beat us. He was respectful to his friends and other people in public, but at home he was a no-good drunk who terrorized his family.

Other people loved my dad — he was always around for them. But when it came to us kids and my mom, I don't remember him ever bein' there for us. What I do remember are the beatings he gave us. I remember *them* clearly. The only dealings I usually had with him, or saw my family havin' with him, were cruel and violent.

My Mom —
The Woman Dad Hit On Became The Woman Dad Hit

My mom's name was Clara Beyer. My dad and my mom's brother, Leo, had served together in the Navy and that's how they met. They were married in February of 1948. Her family had come to this country from Germany in 1939 — just before the war. She was 10 years old at the time.

She was 5'2" and a 110-pound powerhouse. She was our protector. We were her kids and she did everything she knew to save us from our dad, or anyone else she thought mistreated us. Sometimes she'd tease us or make fun of us, but the bottom line was, we were her boys. I adored her.

Mom might have been small, but she was tough and didn't take a whole lot from the old man or anybody else. But he weighed about 200 pounds, and she always wound up on the short end if he decided to take things out on her. There was more than one time that she took a beatin' because of one of us.

All the kids in the neighborhood loved my mom. Our friends used to come over just to hang out with her. She was the life of the party and they loved to be around her. Lots of times they'd come over, and if we weren't there, they'd just stay and hang out with my mom. She always talked to them and usually gave them somethin' to eat.

Both of my parents worked hard, and my mom managed their finances so well that they were eventually able to buy some rental houses and own a successful truckin' business and a tavern of their own. To outsiders, it looked like we had it all — the all-American family.

My Family —
Come On Over And Go a Few Rounds
Neither of my folks seemed to know very much about what it took to make a marriage work or how to discipline kids with love rather than ridicule or anger. Because of this, our house was a war zone.

As my brother Richie put it, the old man began toughenin' us up when we were babies. We never knew when we might be terrorized in the middle of the night — pulled out of our beds and have the crap kicked out of us.

Nobody but our family ever knew what my dad was really like.

Mom would intervene, and she'd get her lights punched out. I don't know how many times I watched my dad smash my mom. She was a fighter, but she could never win.

All they ever did was fight. It was a rotten relationship neither of them should have been in. My mom used to tell us kids that as soon as we were all 18, she was leavin'. But she never got the chance. A year before my youngest brother turned 18 she developed kidney failure and heart problems. She died two years later.

My brother Richie found her on the floor of the apartment she and my dad lived in next to the tavern they owned. Seven days after my mom's death, my dad married his girlfriend, Laurie.

My Brothers and Me
When I was four, Richie and Emil and I were foolin' around in our basement together.

We had a dry well in our basement with about two inches of water in it and Emil was bendin' over playin' in the water. Just as I turned to look, Richie threw a four foot by two inch pole at Emil's rear, but instead of hittin' Emil, the pole hit me in the left eye. The only thing I remember is the incredible pain. I've been told that my entire eyeball came out of the socket and was hangin' by one strand.

My dad heard me screamin' and came runnin' into the basement. When he saw what had happened, he ran past me and began beatin' my brothers — leavin' me to lay there on the steps bleedin' and screamin' in pain. My mom grabbed me and took me to a neighbor's house for help. Our neighbor drove us to the hospital 'cuz my dad was too busy beatin' up my brothers.

Everybody Called Me A Loser —
And I Started Believin' It

I don't remember much of the next two years. The doctors were able to save my eye, but the accident damaged the speech center in my brain. When I entered kindergarten the followin' year nobody could understand what I said. Before the accident I could talk just like everyone else. But now, when I tried to talk, the only thing that came out was gibberish.

Eventually my family was able to understand the meanin' of my words, but nobody else could. Everybody thought I was stupid and dumb because I couldn't talk like other people. What they didn't realize was that I understood everything as well as I ever had — I just wasn't able to say things in a way that they could understand. In fact, my teachers used to have my brothers come into my classroom to interpret what I said.

Kids made fun of me, teachers made fun of me, even my family made fun of me. I was told so often I was stupid that I began to buy into it. I felt like it must be true 'cuz I heard it every day.

In the beginning, I got teased and beat up so much that I withdrew from people and would only hang out with my brothers and a couple of neighborhood kids. My first year at school I was scared and kept to myself. For a long time I went home in tears almost every day.

Battlin' My Way Through School

In first grade, I met a kid by the name of Chuck K. and we became best friends. He was in my speech class because he had a bad stutterin' problem. He stuttered and I couldn't talk. Between the two of us we were pretty messed up but, amazingly, we understood each other. Chuck remained one of my best friends until he joined the Marine Corps after high school.

I Stopped Kissin' Butt And Started Kickin' It

Well, Chuck and I got tired of all the teasin' and started fightin' back. We'd take anybody on and eventually we became really good fighters. If older kids teased us, I told Richie and he'd kick their butts for us. Finally, word got around that it didn't pay to pick on Chuck and me 'cuz it was a guaranteed butt-kickin'. After a while the teasin' pretty much stopped.

I was put in a slow class in school and attended speech classes every day until I was in the eighth grade. I finally quit because it was so humiliating to have someone come into my classroom and announce in front of all the kids that it was time for me to go to speech class.

By the time I was in ninth grade, my speech was pretty much back to normal, but the belief that I was stupid stayed with me. I continued to believe this about myself even after I was able to talk like everybody else. I'd been told so many times what a dumb kid I was that I totally believed it. As a result, I was very angry. I hated myself and I didn't care about other people. I was in trouble so much at school that I had my own favorite chair outside the principal's office — where I ended up at least once a day.

Wisconsin State Chess Champion at Age Nine — Not Bad For A Stupid Loser

My older brothers loved to play chess, and when I was about eight they were the playground champions. Nobody could beat them. I would sit for hours and just watch them play.

After about two months of watchin' their moves I knew the game, so I asked my brothers if I could play. Of course they just laughed at me. These guys and their friends played chess for hours and thought that I was nuts to want to play 'em. But I insisted, so Jeff, one of Emil's friends who was a pretty good player, told me he'd play me.

Emil and Richie watched as I proceeded to kick this kid's butt. It was the first time I ever played the game, but I beat him. He was so sure that it was just luck that he demanded a rematch. So I beat him a second time. Then Richie got on the table and I beat him. And then Emil got on the table and I beat him.

From then on I took on all comers, but nobody on the playground could beat me except Emil and sometimes Richie.

That year our whole playground entered a two day Wisconsin State Chess Championship at Hawthorne Glen Park. Kids eight to eighteen participated, from schools all over the state. I entered the eight- and nine-year-old division.

That first day I was the only one from my playground who didn't lose a match. This meant I was invited to return the next day with my parents to play in the finals. My mom had to work, and my dad wasn't interested in takin' me, so Richie and I hopped on a bus and rode all the way to Hawthorne Glen by ourselves.

I'll never forget Richie standin' over me durin' each game, tellin' me he was gonna hurt me if I didn't hurry up and beat these suckers because he wanted to get home. It must have worked because I didn't lose one game that day, and I became the state chess champion in my age division.

Motivated by my win, I decided to challenge the champion of the 11-12-year-old division. That day I took on and beat most of the state champions in every age division except the 16-18-year-old champion. I think I probably would have beat him too, if we had played.

After that, some guys from a local men's chess club came to the playground and asked me to join their group. They wanted to take me to Chicago and other cities to play, but my folks didn't think it was important and didn't encourage me, so I never went. I continued to play on the playground at school. I even beat the instructors who came around to teach kids how to play.

You know, you'd think that this experience would have helped me know that I wasn't stupid — but it didn't. To my family, chess was just a game; to me it was just a competition. Besides, I figured if somethin' was easy for *me,* it must not be any big deal. I didn't know that it had anything to do with intelligence.

Because so many of the things that my family and other people placed value on (like sittin' still in the classroom when I was bored out of my mind) were hard for me, I figured that if I had beaten all those kids it must not mean very much. At the time, I didn't know that the tests or the letter grades at the top of pages of homework don't always show how smart someone is. I didn't know that there are different learnin' styles, and different ways of bein' smart. All I knew was that I didn't fit in a regular classroom, so I must be stupid. I gave up on myself, and when I was around 12, I stopped playin' chess and started playin' gangster.

My Favorite Memories
Are Of Hangin' With My Brothers

I always felt very close to all of my brothers. Richie, Kenny, and I were the bullies of the neighborhood, especially Richie. My favorite memories are of hangin' out with them playin' baseball, football, and chess. We did a lot together as brothers. For a while we were closer to one another than we were to anyone else. Richie and Emil even taught me how to hunt and fish.

We were a close-knit family, but we were very hard on one another. Violence was a way of life in our house. It was our answer to everything. It was how we played, how we settled arguments, and how we dealt with our anger and frustrations.

In fact, I don't remember a day goin' by when I didn't have a fight with one of my brothers or they weren't fightin' each other. I'm talkin' bloody fights, with fists or bottles or whatever we happened to have in our hands at the time. We were nuts! We all had tempers and would pound the heck out of each other, but ten minutes later we'd forgive each other and go hang out.

We could abuse one another, but we wouldn't let anybody else get between us. I mean it. My friends knew better than to try and step in if I was fightin' with one of my brothers. They knew we'd both stop fightin' each other just long enough to kick *their* butt before we finished our own fight.

Richie — My Protector Was Also My Hero
When I was 11 or 12, I hung around Richie until he wouldn't let me any more. I idolized him. He was my hero. He was cool, smart, and tough. Everybody respected him. Nobody dared to mess with Richie — except the old man.

As the oldest, Richie took more beatings than the rest of us. Everybody got beat up, but Richie got it the worst. My dad would whip him until his back would bleed, but Richie wouldn't ever cry or show my dad that he was hurt in any way. He'd challenge my dad by askin' him, "Is that all you got, old man?" The more my dad beat him, the tougher Richie got. I really hated watchin' them go after one another.

The Fish Got Away — But Richie Didn't
I lived in constant terror because I never knew what would set the old man off. When Richie was about 11 and I was 7 he took us fishin'. What should have been a relaxin' fun day turned into a terrifying experience I'll never forget.

Richie got lucky and hauled in the biggest perch I've ever seen caught in that lake. This fish was huge and, boy, were we excited. Richie carefully reeled it in, but when he got it into the boat the fish started wriggling in his hands, flopped back into the water, and got away. We tried to get it, but we were too late. My dad went crazy. He doubled up his fist and smashed Richie square in the face. He cold-cocked an 11-year-old kid just for losin' a stupid fish.

I remember thinkin' that there was no way I was gonna catch

any fish for fear of losin' it at the boat. That day, any time I got a bite, the fish bobbed on the line as many times as it wanted to. I wasn't about to try and haul it up into the boat.

My Hero Goes To Prison

The first time Richie went to prison, he was 14 and I was 10. I'll always remember the day the cops dragged him away.

My brother Emil and I had a paper route. I can still see us goin' out that Sunday mornin' to deliver our papers and bein' surrounded by the cops. Emil tried to explain to them that they were lookin' for our brother Richie, not us. They didn't care and made us lie face down in the snow with shotguns to our heads.

Here we were, 10 and 12 years old, and the cops had shotguns to our heads. We finally convinced them that neither of us were Richie and they let us up. We let them into the house and they woke up Richie. Of course he denied knowin' what they were talkin' about.

It took the cops about thirty minutes before they found the $240 he'd stolen, stashed under Emil's pillow, and they finally dragged him away. He'd been in and out of juvenile detention centers from the time he was 12, but this was his first serious bust.

Richie got sent away for two years. I was so mad at him for leavin' me home all alone. This was to be the beginnin' of Richie's long career of drugs, crime, and doin' time. Years later he told me that he kept gettin' locked up so he wouldn't have to go through all the crap he had to deal with at our house. As a kid he felt safer in the joint than he did in his own home.

Today he's got a good job and a supportive lady. Not long ago he told me that for the first time in his life he's content and happy.

Emil — The Black Sheep Of The Family

Richie, Kenny, and I were always in trouble with the law. It's interesting to me that even though all of us were smart kids, Emil was the only one of us who made healthy choices early in his life.

He was the white knight of the family — or the black sheep, whichever way you want to look at it. He was the only one of us who didn't get in trouble with the cops, the only one of us who didn't go to jail, and, until a few years ago, the only one of us who went to college.

In the early years we used to have a lot of fun playin' ball and chess together, but once Richie and I started gettin' into serious trouble, Emil stopped hangin' out with us. School was his sanctuary, and teachers became his heroes. His love of learning helped him to make different choices than the rest of us, but it didn't make it any less painful for him to be at home.

You'd think that our dad would've been very proud of Emil because he never got into trouble and did so well in school. But nothin' Emil did was ever good enough for the old man. No matter what, there just wasn't any pleasin' him.

It wasn't until I was in my thirties and was out of the dope business that Emil and I finally got close again. I'm glad he was able to make the choices he made as a kid and didn't go through what the rest of us did. Today he's a teacher and a wonderful husband and father.

Kenny — The Smartest Criminal I Ever Knew

My brother Kenny was probably the most criminally brilliant, and the most out of control, of all of us. Even though he was the youngest, he was really tough. After all, he grew up with Richie and me beatin' him up almost every day. He was our scapegoat. He was also my best friend.

As kids we were inseparable. You couldn't be his friend unless you were my friend; and you couldn't be my friend unless you were his friend. We did everything together until I was 12 or 13. After that we still stayed best friends, but didn't hang out together as much.

Kenny was a brilliant kid who hated school, but loved to work on cars and motorcycles. He was a mechanical genius. His dream was to own the fastest car in Milwaukee. He owned a Roadrunner, and had souped it up pretty good, but there was another car that used to run at the Milwaukee race track that had a 426 Hemmy in it.

Now this engine was worth a lot of money and Kenny wanted it. So he went all the way to Chicago, found out where the car was bein' kept, and stole it. He brought it back to Milwaukee, and by the end of the night had the whole car stripped and cut into pieces. He kept the parts he needed and got rid of the rest.

For many years Kenny had one of the fastest cars in town. It was awesome how fast this car really was. It was so fast the force would jerk your head back when he took off, and there was no way you could bring your head forward.

When Kenny was 19 years old he joined the Heaven's Devils motorcycle gang. That year he was killed in a high-speed motorcycle chase with the cops. To this day, Kenny is the closest friend I've ever had. Twenty-five years later I still think about him and miss him a lot.

Kenny Wasn't Big, But He Was More Than Crazy Enough To Make Up For It

Kenny had an incredible temper, and an attitude to match. It was plain stupid to mess with him. We had a cousin who, at 225 pounds, was one bad dude. One day he and Kenny were at our bar playin' pool and my cousin wouldn't stop messin' with him. Kenny kept tellin' him to leave him alone, but the guy just wouldn't quit.

So Kenny got the shotgun from behind the bar and blew the windows out of his brand new truck. My cousin went runnin' out as soon as he heard the shotgun blast and Kenny put the gun to this guy's mouth and said, "You're next if you try to jerk me around again." Even though he was older and bigger, my cousin never messed with Kenny again.

He went to Black River Falls when he was 15 years old. It was a Boy's Home — one of the tougher ones. One thing about going to jail: you have the opportunity to develop new skills and trades. When he was at Black River Falls somebody taught him how to break a lock, and Kenny perfected the technique until he could get past any lock around — a safe or anything else.

Kenny was the kind of guy who would do anything on a dare or bet. Right before he was killed there was a big fire at Times Square, a local shoppin' center. One of the stores happened to be a men's shop that sold nothin' but beautiful leather coats. It was a very exclusive store. Twenty-five years ago their coats sold for $250 to $500.

My brother saw this place and made a bet with some friends that he could get into the store without gettin' caught. Now the cops had a 24-hour patrol around that store, so his friends figured this was gonna be an easy bet. They should've known better.

Kenny got up on the roof and made a hole in it, and he and a friend climbed from the roof down into the store and grabbed about 200 fur coats and leather jackets, put them in boxes, and took them out through the roof.

Durin' the robbery, the cops came to check things out, and Kenny and his friend had to hide for about 35 minutes before they finally left. Kenny didn't get caught. The cops never knew it was him. He died before he could get rid of all the merchandise, so for years afterward we all had plenty of beautiful suede and leather coats.

Kenny was very good at what he did. He only got caught twice — the time he was sent to Black River Falls and the day he died.

When Kenny died, part of me died with him.

Things I Think About

- *The beatings and dysfunction were well-kept secrets in our family.*
- *When I was a kid I didn't know how to face the pain and isolation I felt. I got tough so no one could hurt me. Back then, I didn't know there was another way out.*

CHAPTER 4

PLAYIN' GANGSTER:
My Juvenile Criminal Career

Grow Up To Be President?
Not When I Could Be a Gangster

Growin' up, all I ever wanted to be was a gangster. They were my heroes. Not Presidents of the United States, but gangsters like John Dillinger, Al Capone, and Jesse James. These guys were smart, powerful, and respected. Nobody bullied them.

When I turned 12, I was on the street day and night. I hated school and was only there when I had to be. I was on suspension almost as much as I was in class. The only times I saw my dad durin' those years was when he'd have to get me back in school.

More Suspensions Than The Golden Gate Bridge

When we were 15, Chuck and Kruno and I set records for the number of suspensions per semester. When the school called my parents, I'd go, but after a few days I'd be right back out there, hangin' and fightin' with the Burleigh and 95th Street Boys. We were into everything: assault and battery, car theft, burglary, and extortion.

In the beginning, my folks blamed Kruno and tried to make me stay away from him. They were like so many parents today who refuse to admit their kids could do these things. After awhile, they woke up. By the time Kenny came along they didn't look for other kids to blame.

Extortion: The Criminal Empire
Built On Lunch Money

One day, my friends and I decided that we were tired of not havin' any money, so we decided to go into the collections and protection business. We'd stop kids on the way to school, convince them that it was in their best interest to pay us to protect them, and we'd take their lunch money.

On special occasions, like homecomin' dances and proms, we'd collect $2-$5 per couple, dependin' on what they had in their pocket. We were the bullies moms always warn their kids about. One night we collected over $100. When I was a kid, that was pretty good money.

A New Set Of Brothers —
Chuck K., Kruno, And Me

Chuck K. and I had been best friends for a long time when we met Kruno. We were about 12 or 13 at the time. Some punk at school tried to get Kruno to beat me up. But when Kruno saw me and Richie he told the guy, "Forget it, you do him." We left friends.

Chuck and I were buddies until he joined the Marines right after high school. But Kruno and I were brothers until he was killed. We went through a lot of stuff together. From the day we met we were true partners in crime. Kruno was the kind of guy who would have given his life for me. I knew I could always count on him no matter what.

The Burleigh Boys: Not Exactly The Boy Scouts

When I was 12, we started hangin' out with a local gang called The Burleigh Boys, and our criminal career began for real. That year we graduated from stealing booze and chump change from other kids to stealing cars and burglarizin' houses. We were the exception to the rule. Back then gangs weren't in every small town in America like they are today.

The Burleigh Boys became my family. We never really had a leader — there were a lot of us who thought we were real bad and we just hung out. At first there were only about 30 of us, but we developed a reputation, and at our height there were around 50 to 60 kids, includin' the wannabe's.

First Time I Stole a Car: A Smashing Experience

I'll never forget our first attempt at stealin' a car. I had just turned 13. A few of us were hangin' out and decided we wanted to go for a ride, so we went to a local church parkin' lot, found a car with the keys in it, and stole it. The problem was, it was a stick shift and none of us had driven anything but an automatic. We must have banged into ten or fifteen cars tryin' to get out of that parking lot. We all took a turn tryin' to drive the car, 'cuz each of us figured we could do better than the other guy. Boy, were we wrong.

Here we were in a church parkin' lot at 11:30 on a Sunday morning smashin' into all those cars like we were at a demolition derby, and nobody seemed to hear us. I've never seen so many cars mangled in such a short time in my whole life. I'm not kiddin' you, none of us knew how to drive. We finally got about four blocks from the church and said, "Forget this, let's go find an automatic."

After that, we got smart. We went to a local junk yard and learned how to drive. In those days they kept the keys right in the junkers and some of them would still run. Eventually we got tired of playin' demolition derby in the junk yard and started stealin' cars for real.

My First Used Car Dealership
That year we had one of the biggest car theft rings in the city and probably set a police record. We began takin' orders. We'd steal cars and sell them to other kids for $10 or $15. That may not sound like serious money to you, but I was makin' $200 to $300 a week. For a 13-year-old that was a lot of money.

On cold winter mornings we'd cruise the neighborhood and watch for a car warmin' up in some poor sucker's driveway. One of us would jump out and drive off in the car. There were plenty of mornings when some out-of-shape middle-aged guy would drop his morning coffee and come chasin' and cussin' after us as we drove off in his nice new car.

The other place we found easy pickins was used car lots. Back then, car dealers often left the keys in the ignition all night. All we had to do was drop by and drive off.

You'd Have Thought This Was My First Burglary
It didn't take us long to graduate from auto theft to burglary. We used to rip off stores in Milwaukee that sold hardware, huntin' gear, and clothes. Once a month we'd nail a semi parked at a loadin' dock. Most of the time we'd get lawn furniture and stuff that was easy to get rid of.

This time my buddies and I decided that instead of just loadin' up our cars, it'd be easier to take the whole truck. We took our time, and planned the job carefully. We knew where we were gonna unload, and how we were gonna move the merchandise. The day came and we were ready!

Well, we got that semi, and drove it out to a deserted area we knew of in the country. The rest of the team was out there waitin' to help us unload. You can't believe the shock we got when we opened up the semi and saw what we had. There must have been 10,000 toilet seats in the back of the trailer. At first we were mad, but after a few minutes, Chuck started laughin', then Kruno and Kenny and then me. We laughed so hard I thought we'd wet our pants. We finally stopped laughin' long enough to take the semi back and leave it in the parkin' lot.

On Weekends I Went To Jail
Like Other Kids Go To The Mall
Between stealin' cars and burglarizin' houses and stores, we stayed busy and always had plenty of money in our pockets.

But eventually we started gettin' busted. After a while, it became a weekly affair. For six months, I was arrested about every weekend, for assault and battery, car theft, or strong-armed robbery. The only thing I never got caught for was burglary.

I didn't mind goin' to jail because half the kids there were members of my gang. In fact, I liked bein' at the Juvenile Detention Center better than I liked bein' at home. It was more like a recreational thing. At least I wasn't in danger of gettin' beat up by the old man while I was in jail. Besides, we ran the place. I even had my own special bed. It was my home away from home.

Doin' Hard Time: It Wasn't Fun Anymore
For two years I was in and out of the detention center almost every weekend. It was a revolvin' door for me.

Then, when I was fifteen, I was on probation when Kruno and I got busted again for auto theft. By this time the judge was sick of seein' us in his courtroom. We'd been in and out of his jail probably 50 times in the past two years and he'd had it with us.

I'll never forget that day. My mom and dad were both in the courtroom. Kruno went before the judge first, and the judge asked him if he thought he could straighten out if he were given one final chance.

Kruno looked at him and said, "Screw you!"

I was shocked. Here the judge was actually givin' him a chance to choose the streets or jail, and he chose jail.

When it was my turn, he looked at me and asked, "Well, what about you?"

I looked at my dad and saw the anger in his eyes. For me, this was a hard decision. I didn't want to go home to the beatin' my dad was gonna give me, but I wanted to stay out of jail for my mom's sake because I could see that she was takin' this real hard. So I looked at the judge and asked him if he could give me a minute to think about it.

That judge must've thought I was bein' a smartalec. He immediately revoked my probation and sent me to Wales Youth Home for Boys.

I wasn't there long before I received a reputation for being a troublemaker and was informed that I was bein' transferred to Flambeau, a medium-security adult work camp. Up until that time, juveniles in Wisconsin hadn't been put in this type of adult prison.

Let me tell you, this wasn't fun any more. In fact, it was downright scary. Here we were with murderers and other hardened criminals. Six or seven kids, ages 14 to 16, had been sent to Flambeau, and we all hung together. Durin' the day we chopped trees and did other work for the forestry department. In the fall, us kids were supposed to attend classes at a local high school — but I never made it. Instead they sent me back to

Wales.

Race Riots And Murder

I was never officially told why I was transferred, but I figured it was because they thought I witnessed a stabbin'. Race riots were going' on back in Milwaukee. Everybody in the joint had heard about them. The violence spilled over into the prison and a black guy ended up gettin' stabbed. I never knew if he lived or died.

I'd been in the area when the stabbin' took place, so the prison authorities questioned me about it. Everybody knew what had happened, but there was no way I was gonna rat these guys out. I didn't want to wake up dead.

Back To Wales

A couple of days later I was told to get my things together because I was going somewhere. It turned out they were takin' me to the hole. After 24 hours the guards came and shackled me, and put me and my friend Tommy on a bus back to Wales.

At Wales, I figured they would take me out of the shackles and put me back into the general population. Was I wrong! I was immediately taken to the hole, where I stayed for a week. While I was in the hole my mom came to see me. She asked me what was goin' on, and I told her that I didn't know — and I didn't. I never did figure out why they kept me in the hole.

A week later I was brought before the Review Board on some charges I didn't know anything about. Once again I got labeled a troublemaker and had several extra months tacked onto my sentence. This time I was told that I was bein' transferred to the juvenile facility at Plymouth.

Before it was over, I spent time in three different prisons. The whole experience left me bitter toward the system. I'd had a chip on my shoulder since I was little, but this made it much worse.

When I finally got out on parole, I promised my mom I'd never go back again.

I Went Straight — Straight Into The Army

I met my future wife, Linda, just before I went to jail. She wrote a friend of mine while I was in the joint and asked about me. When I got home I saw her at a dance and we started hangin' out. Soon we began datin'.

Linda was beautiful and very smart, a real classy girl. She did my homework every day and coached me before tests. If it hadn't been for her I wouldn't have made it through high school.

Bein' with Linda helped keep me straight. I still used a lot of drugs, and got high every day, but I quit stealin' cars and burglarizin' houses, and pretty much stayed out of trouble.

Then, a few weeks before I was supposed to graduate from high school, I was hangin' out with some friends. One of the guys with us had just broken up with his girlfriend and was drunk out of his mind. The more he drank, the crazier he got. As we walked past a hardware store he went berserk and kicked out their plate glass window. Of course, the alarm started goin' off and people on the street saw all of us run to my car. Somebody in the crowd wrote down my license plate number, and when I got home that night the cops were waitin' for me.

My parole officer suspected I hadn't done it, but he got really ticked off when I refused to tell him who had. It was such a stupid thing, but he got mad and pulled my parole. I was on my way back to prison.

I was sittin' in his office and he said, "Look, Ron, you have a choice. I'm sending you back to prison, or you can join the Army." I figured I'd already been to jail so many times, I might as well try the Army.

As it turned out, my parole officer was an officer in the Wisconsin Army National Guard. He'd already made arrangements for me to join the Guard. This won't mean much to you, but this was the height of the Vietnam war and it nearly took an act of Congress to get into the National Guard. There was a waitin' list a mile long of medical and law students tryin' to get in.

On the last day of school, I was put on a plane to Ft. Jackson, South Carolina, for Army basic trainin'. I didn't even get to walk across the stage to pick up my diploma. My mom went up and picked it up for me.

The very first day off the bus, my wallet — with all my money in it —got stolen. I thought, "Ain't this somethin'. Here I am with car theft rings and burglary rings in Milwaukee, and my first day in the Army some crazy dude steals my wallet!"

I called home and told my mom, and she said that she would send me some cash. I told her I didn't need her money, that I'd handle it.

I went on a rampage. I'd made friends with some guys from Puerto Rico and we hit every locker in Ft. Jackson. By the end of the first week we had all the money we wanted.

CHAPTER 5

Payin' My Dues

I Tried To Go Straight

I promised my mom I wouldn't go back to jail, so when I got back from basic trainin' I stayed straight and hung out with Linda.

Around this time I got my first Harley — a 1943 Knucklehead. It was in a million pieces when I found it, but a friend of mine rebuilt it for me, and when he got finished it was a classic.

I was friends with, and rode with, guys from the Heaven's Devils and the Milwaukee Chapter of the Outlaws, but never officially joined either club. Kenny joined the Heaven's Devils, but I never wanted to go through the b.s. they put you through durin' probation. The only authority I wanted to answer to was my own.

I tried workin' at different jobs, but didn't like any of them. My mom and dad had bought a tavern in West Allis, on Milwaukee's south side, and they asked me and Kenny to work as bartenders. Kenny took the day shift and I worked nights and weekends.

Kenny's Death Left Me Empty Inside

Things were pretty good for awhile. Then my grandfather died, and two weeks later Kenny got killed in a high-speed motorcycle chase with the Milwaukee police. My grandfather was old and had been sick a long time, so his death didn't come as a surprise. But when Kenny was killed I went into shock. I did anything I could to numb the pain. I got drunk or high just about every day. I started messin' around with a lot of the women who came into the bar.

From The Bar To The Brewery

I didn't want to lose one more person in my life, so in order to save my marriage I quit the bar and went to work for Coca-Cola®. I loved it because I was outside. But there really wasn't much of a future for me at Coca Cola, so I started lookin' for another job.

Eventually I moved on to a higher payin' job at Dolly Madison. I worked for Dolly Madison for what turned out to be one of the worst years of my life. The job sucked. I started my route at 4:30 every mornin' and usually didn't get home until five or six every night. This definitely was not the way I wanted to spend the rest of my life.

I'd been goin' to Pabst every week for a year, buggin' the guy to give me a job, and it finally paid off. They put me in the factory for two months, and then a truck drivin' job came open and I began my delivery route. Things were gettin' better.

From Beer To Drugs In One Layoff

Not long after I started my new job, I got caught in a big layoff at Pabst. I knew there was no way I could take care of my family on unemployment, so I began lookin' for ways to supplement my income until Pabst called me back to work.

The Choice: Flippin' Dope Or Sellin' Amway

Believe it or not, I actually considered gettin' involved in multilevel marketing sellin' Amway. A friend of mine kept tellin' me how much money I could make, and Linda and I really did seriously think about joinin' the company. There've been times I've looked back over the past 15 years and wondered what my life would've been like today if I'd gone into Amway instead of the dope business.

Amway Loses

One day I was pickin' up some marijuana and happened to mention that I'd been laid off. The guy I was buyin' from said, "Ron, for years you've been dabblin' in the dope business. Why don't you get serious and make some real money? With all the people you know, it'd be easy for you to build a nice little business."

For as long as I could remember I'd been buyin' a quarter pound of marijuana a week. I'd sell three ounces to friends for the price I'd paid for the quarter pound and then I'd smoke my ounce for free. It was just somethin' I did to pay for my dope. I'd never really considered gettin' into the business for real.

I told him I'd think about it, and went home and talked it over with Linda. It took us about a week to make the decision. At first, we figured that we could do this to get by until I got called back to Pabst. Besides, I told myself it'd give me a little extra time to spend with my family.

We took $1750 of our savings and bought five pounds of pot at $350 a pound. What happened next blew everybody's mind. Linda and I figured that it would take us about a month to get rid of the five pounds, but the stuff was gone in three days. It took only a week to collect all our money. I made more money that week than I would have made workin' a whole month at Pabst.

I was hooked. It was just too easy! But nobody told me how hard it was really gonna be to keep friends and make money in this business. I thought life was gonna be a breeze.

Blinded by greed, I figured all I'd have to do was sit home and count my money. I didn't count on the tens of thousands of dollars I'd lose when one of my mules got busted or killed. I didn't count on the hundreds of thousands of dollars and the number of friends and business associates I'd lose because they got wasted by the competition or caught in a DEA sting.

The Dope Business — It's More Of a Business Than I Thought

I went from sellin' five pounds to 50 pounds in two weeks, and from 50 pounds to 200 pounds in another 12 weeks. I started undercuttin' the competition by $25 a pound and soon had more people than I could easily handle. I'd grown so fast that I had to find a way to get things under control. It was nuts. I had people comin' and goin' from my house at all hours. The phone rang constantly. It was almost like I had a neon sign in front of my house sayin', "Ron's Drug Store." I didn't have a minute to myself.

Creatin' My Network

This wasn't my idea of a life. Sellin' dope was supposed to make things easier, not harder. I'd never worked such long hours in my life. Somethin' had to give.

One of the reasons that my business had grown so quickly was that my supplier had turned some of his customers over to me. I reasoned that I could do the same with my customers. I had already been ripped off a couple of times and I realized that the more people I dealt with directly, the greater the chances of somethin' goin' wrong.

I quit flippin' ounces and pounds and required a five-pound minimum for anybody to even think of gettin' it from me. I chose my strongest, most trustworthy guys and told them that if they would buy only from me, I would send them customers and help them develop their businesses. It worked great. Eventually I was dealin' with only five top guys. Everybody else was under them.

The Danger Of Moving And Storing Dope

I knew I wouldn't make as much money sellin' in volume as I could have made if I sold directly to all the nickel and dimers, but it cut down on the problems and risks — or so I thought. Actually, I just traded one set of headaches for another — transportin' and storage.

I always made sure when I was gettin' in a big shipment that it would be gone in a day or two — in the front door and right out the back. I never sat on a shipment.

I knew a couple of straight family-type guys from Pabst who had barns and garages. They let me rent them for a couple of days when the pot first came into town. Mainly I kept my stash on a farm. These guys weren't dealers or into drugs at all. They were just straitlaced Pabst people. People I knew I could trust.

I liked to work with these guys because they weren't criminals and they weren't users, so I didn't have to worry about the cops lookin' for them. They were just good family men who could use some extra cash. They made $250 a week at Pabst, and I paid them $500 a week if I needed to stash some of my dope with them.

As soon as a shipment came in, I'd take a couple of the guys out to the farm. We'd weigh it and get it out of there. I hated to warehouse my dope, and I wouldn't do it unless I had to. I always had three main guys who were willin' to take 300 to 500 pounds each, and the rest went out in smaller amounts.

By this time I'd met Billy and Pete, who eventually became my main suppliers. They had great connections. Not only did we do lot of business together, we became close friends. I trusted them and they knew they could trust me.

My business had grown to the point that semi-loads of marijuana were comin' into town just for me. We never brought it in the same way twice. Sometimes we'd send a senior citizen to Florida or Mexico for a few days vacation, and then have them drive a motor home back to Milwaukee loaded down with my dope. This was the early days of the dope business, and the old folks never got stopped.

This Trip To Mexico Was No Vacation
It was harder gettin' dope into the country than it was gettin' it home to Milwaukee. *Anything could happen, and a lot of times it did.* Some weeks I lost more money than I made. I learned the hard way that in this business, if somethin' bad *can* happen, eventually it does.

I'll never forget the time Billy, Pete, and I were bringin' 10,000 pounds of pot out of Mexico. We had hired a pilot to bring it into the country for us. Billy went along with him, and Pete and I waited on the ground. They were supposed to be landin' in a safe location, but the pilot ran out of gas and had to land in another field about ten miles from where we originally planned to meet them.

Let me tell you, this was one mistake that almost cost the pilot his life. If he'd bothered to check the gas gauges and had filled the gas tanks like he'd been told, none of this would ever have happened. The guy nearly blew a million-dollar deal because of a lousy tank of fuel.

Billy radioed ahead to warn us about what was goin' down and we met them in a big farm field. As soon as the pilot stepped out of the plane, Pete was on him. He dropped the guy on the spot, knocking out some of his teeth and breaking his nose before we stopped him. If we hadn't pulled Pete off of him, he probably would've pistol whipped the guy to death.

Of course the farmer came out to find out what was goin' on and ended up with a gun to his head. We quickly explained the situation to him. We lucked out — he turned out to be a cool guy. He helped us unload and even invited us to eat dinner with him and his family, and told us that any time we ever needed to land there again we could. You should've seen the look on the farmer's face when Pete handed him $10,000 for lookin' out for us. This was one time, despite problems, that things worked out, and I got my share of the load to take back to Milwaukee.

You Can't Sell Dope You Don't Have
Good business is built around supply and demand, and although there was always a demand for good marijuana, the supply was seasonal. It was only available certain times of the year. I found out that if I was gonna depend only on my marijuana business, I would starve all summer. The peak season was September through February. Come February or March, availability dropped and prices could double. People who are willin' to warehouse until February or March could really clean up. I never wanted to hold on to it that long, but I knew people who did.

If I could get some good stuff during the summer months, I could always get rid of it. But the availability was very uncertain and there were many dry periods. Things would be goin' really good, then the supply would dry up. It drove me nuts.

Durin' one of these dry spells, I gave a guy I thought was my friend $15,000 for a business deal. He walked out on me. In fact, he burned me and eight other people in Milwaukee. It was January and there was no marijuana to be found. Nothin' was goin' on. I was laid off from Pabst, I'd just lost all the ready cash I had, and I was gonna have to start all over.

Cocaine — A New Market For Idiots With Money

Some guys I knew happened to drop by. After findin' out what had just happened, they asked me why I didn't consider flippin' coke. "You've got an incredible network, and lots of people love coke."

I figured, why not? The first couple of years I was in the business I never touched the stuff. Actually, I thought people who did coke were idiots. I couldn't understand how anybody could buy a gram of coke for $90, snort it up their nose, and be done with it two hours later. Ninety dollars meant more to me than that.

I started in the cocaine business pretty much the same way I had the marijuana business. I bought an eight ball and sold three and a half grams, then bought another eight ball, and sold three and a half grams.

I thought, "This is easy." So I bought an ounce. My supplier showed me how to cut it so I'd have an ounce and a quarter. In two nights, I had $500 in my pocket.

Two months later I was flippin' a kilo a month. In my heyday I sometimes sold as much as three to five pounds a month. I started off small, and pretty soon everybody I knew loved cocaine and wanted to get into the business. I started them out small and they grew with me.

I trained my people just like one of my suppliers had trained me. When I first started sellin' coke, my supplier invested a lot of time in teachin' me the finer points of the business. By the time I graduated from his academy of fine coke, I was a true professional.

He made sure I knew how to tell high-grade powder and rock

from the crap you usually find on the street. He taught me how to cut my coke with speed, mannitol, and other fillers in a way that fooled even some of my best customers. There's a lot of people out there who've been doin' or sellin' a little coke and think they're coke connoisseurs, but they don't know jack about how things really work. I could sell 'em some rock I'd made and they'd swear it was the best they'd ever tasted.

I was good at what I did and taught my dealers what I had learned. Back then, 90% of the people into cocaine didn't know what they were really buyin'. They didn't know that they were gettin' mostly speed and cut.

Why Do You Think They Call 'Em Deadbeats?

There's only two ways bad debts are forgiven on the street: if you're dead or if you lose the money in a bust and are willin' to quietly do the time. Otherwise, when you owe somebody, you pay no matter what. Whether you get ripped off or lose the money in a bad deal, it doesn't matter. You work it out and pay what you owe.

A few years back, one of my dealers was havin' a hard time collectin' on a big debt owed to him. As a result, my man couldn't pay me what he owed me. I carried him for a while, but then we heard this deadbeat had started buyin' dope from other suppliers. He never even thought about payin' his debt. He was the kind of guy who always liked to showboat. We knew he was spendin' a lot of money on women, new cars, jewelry, and anything else he wanted. Because of this, he put himself and his family in deep jeopardy.

Since he owed my man, he owed me. I decided it was pay day.

We forced one of his friends to tell us when he was gettin' in a big shipment and I set up the hit. I asked my brother and T.J. to meet me at Perkins Pancake House and told them about the setup. Richie owed me about $10,000 at the time, and I told him I'd call us even if he and T.J. took care of this collection for me.

I'd spent about a week casin' the deadbeat's house and had learned that he left for work every mornin' about 8:00. That meant that by 8:05 his wife would be home alone with his kids. Alot of innocent family members get hurt or die because some player thinks he's invincible.

Richie and T.J. drove to Arlington Heights and waited for the punk to leave for work. As soon as he was gone, they knocked on the front door. When the wife opened the door, they stuck a gun in her face and dragged her into the bathroom — where they tied her up and put duct tape over her mouth.

They came away with $60,000 worth of pot and $25,000 worth of cocaine. We later learned that they missed $100,000 the guy had stashed in one of his dresser drawers. But I didn't mind. My man was able to save face and pay me what he owed me, so we were all happy. I figured $85,000 wasn't bad pay for a couple of hours work.

Buildin' My Empire
Once I figured out that cocaine was always available, I decided to handle both cocaine and marijuana. I liked the coke because it was so much easier to transport and store and there was a greater potential to make big money. But with the increased potential came increased risk. Even back then cops and judges were harder on you if you dealt coke. It became more and more important to have a tightly knit group of dependable people around me.

I developed a close group of brothers who'd do anythin' for me. They'd lay down their lives for me. I had people who, for $15,000, were willin' to take a first-time bust for me. They knew they'd walk away with $15,000 and probation.

I had other guys I could give $25-30,000 worth of merchandise or cash, come back three weeks later or even three years later, and they'd still have it, untouched.

I also had a group of guys — Hit Man, Psycho, and Skid Row — who I knew would go to war for me or hit people if I asked them to. I'd never ask them to hold merchandise or cash, but if I needed a collection made, or if there was the hint of any trouble, there was nobody any better. I could always depend on them or my brother Richie to watch my back.

From Buddies To Bodyguards

There are folks willin' to risk a lot of craziness to get you when they think you're carryin' $100,000 worth of blow or cash. I was careful not to tell people when I was gettin' a shipment in, but it's hard to always keep things like that quiet.

After I started usin' coke I got so paranoid about the threat of bein' ripped off that if someone saw me in a bar and wanted to talk to me, they'd often have to come through my bodyguards first. I always had Kruno, Skid the Kid, Richie, or Rocky positioned to watch my back. Eventually I never went anywhere without at least one bodyguard.

Movin' To The Suburbs

After a few years in the business, I finally had a little money set aside. We had two kids, Linda was pregnant again, and we were livin' in the small two bedroom house my mom had given me. It was time to move into a bigger home. I sold our house so we'd have a nice down payment.

I bought a three bedroom house on an acre of land in an upper-middle-class suburb of Milwaukee. It had a three-car garage and a swimmin' pool. Linda had not been real happy about my flippin' coke. She didn't like the life-style that went along with it. I can't say I blame her. She had three babies to take care of. Our other house had been broken into several times, and she lived in terror that somethin' would happen to the kids. The new house helped to get her off my back for a while.

A Day In The Life Of A Dope Dealer

I worked a straight job at Pabst Brewery and flipped dope six days a week. Weekdays I'd get up every morning at six and do my city deliveries. I took beer to taverns and dope to my friends between runs. Along the way I spent a lot of time at pay phones settin' up deals. I was married to my beeper.

At 3:30 in the afternoon, I'd get home from my day job, take a shower, change my clothes, strap on my guns, and hit the streets to start my real job — dealin'. On a normal day I'd get 25 to 50 calls. It was hard work. I never saw my kids and wouldn't even eat dinner with my wife.

I'd get home between midnight and 3 a.m. At 6 a.m. I'd snort a line of coke to get goin' and do it all over again. That was the routine every week up to Saturday night.

I worked at least 15 to 16 hours a day — sometimes even more. I always figured I had better take care of my people and their demands or they'd find a new supplier.

Trapped In A Vicious Cycle Of Greed

I was driven to make as much money as quickly as I could. I knew I couldn't go on like this forever, so I figured that I'd better "make hay while the sun shines." This was my old man's favorite saying and I lived by it.

Saturday night and Sunday I rested so I could begin again Monday. It's a business, and you have to think of it as a business. If you're thinkin' of it in any other way, you're gonna get caught. You have to be seriously focused or you're gonna blow it.

In the beginning I had thought that this would be just an easy way to make some extra cash and allow me to spend more time with my family. I had told myself that I would quit after my first $100,000, but I got trapped in a vicious cycle of greed. I didn't have time to play husband, father, or happy homeowner because I was too busy chasin' the next big deal.

I had everything I ever thought I wanted — a gorgeous wife, great kids, a beautiful house in the suburbs with a swimmin' pool, cars, motorcycles — and I had no time to enjoy them.

My life was already out of control, but I didn't know it.

Things I Think About

- *Sometimes I wonder what my life would've been like if we'd invested our savings in Amway products instead of pot.*

CHAPTER 6

Groupies, Lawyers
and
Junkies

Livin' On The Edge

I'd always been somebody who lived on the edge, so in the beginning I bought into the romance and mystique so often associated with big-time drug dealers. I loved the drama, the game, and the sense of power you get when you know you're really gettin' over on another person or the system. At first it was fun playin' gangster.

But the glamor died after I sent a friend to Florida with $100,000 and he was found floatin' face down in the Atlantic with a bullet in his brain.

That first year I'd make some good money and then lose it — make some more money and then lose it. I stayed in the business because the potential amount of money I could make on each deal was phenomenal. But this ain't a business where you can expect a UPS delivery every week.

The unpredictability of supply can be a safeguard for the guys who bring the stuff into the country, but it's a headache for the hometown distributor and dealers. People get killed for not bringin' the deal in when they say they're gonna.

I always had to realize that my next shipment was never a sure thing. Somebody could get busted or killed or ripped off. It was a very frustratin' business, and I had to develop a high tolerance for drama and stress. It was like walkin' on the razor's edge — knowin' I could lose everything overnight. I learned very quickly to lighten up and developed an easy-come, easy-go attitude. I had to become calloused to my losses or they'd have driven me crazy.

During my second year in the business, I started flippin' coke and began to make money on a regular basis. I'd been used to makin' $250 a week at the brewery, and here I was bringin' in at least $5,000 a week — when the good dope was available. This was a lot of money, but I spent a lot, too. My overhead was high — what with money lost on bad deals or deals that didn't come in on time, busts, legal fees, and rip-offs, not to mention the profits my friends and I snorted.

Buyin' Legal Insurance

Unlike most of the guys I knew, the very first thing I did when I started in the business was to set aside enough money to buy the best legal protection possible. My lawyer was my most important investment.

Originally, I assumed I'd use this money if I ever got busted. However, it didn't take me long to realize that my legal fund would need to be available to just about everybody in my network. I figured it was good business to provide money for bail and top legal fees to the people who worked for me. It saved me from many sleepless nights wonderin' if one of my guys was gonna rat me out.

I'd been to jail enough times to know I sure wasn't gonna trust my future to some court-appointed lawyer. I'd learned long ago that when you're standin' in front of a judge, the lawyer standin' next to you had better be on a first-name basis with the judge and District Attorney. It's even better if they're well liked and socializes with at least one of them. A top-notch lawyer makes all the difference in the world, and I was willin' to pay whatever price necessary to get the best.

The old saying, "You get what you pay for," is especially true when it comes to lawyers. I paid, but I was never sorry.

The Good News — You Get Cash
The Bad News — You Can't Spend It

Fortunately, my wife was very understandin' when it came to spendin' money. She knew we couldn't risk livin' the high life. Don't get me wrong, she had nice things in her house, and plenty of nice clothes — but she was a smart woman and didn't expect the ridiculous. We had a nice life, but we didn't overdo it.

Eventually my money had no more value than monopoly money because I couldn't really do anything with it. It wasn't real. It was easy money — it was dirty money. A lot of it came and went through my fingers, but it stopped havin' any meaning for me. It was just part of a game I was playin'. Some days I'd win and other days I'd lose the whole bank. It didn't matter be-cause there was always that next big deal.

I tried investin' in a couple legitimate businesses, but I didn't have the time to run them because I was too busy runnin' my dope business. As a result, everything I invested in lost money.

Towards the end, money became my answer to everything. I started payin' my wife to keep her quiet and off my back. I used to give her money just so she would leave me alone. Pretty soon all she expected from me was money — which was a good thing, because at that point I didn't have anything else to give her.

Seduced By The Lady
I want you to know that I didn't taste coke for about the first two years I was in business. Then one night one of my suppliers suggested that I find out what all the fuss was about.

I was shocked at the incredible feelin' that it gave me. I'd been gettin' high for fifteen years, but nothin' had ever come close to the intense pleasure and well-being I experienced the first time I did coke. This stuff was dynamite. It was beyond anything I could've ever imagined.

I started partyin' that night at seven and didn't stop until about four o'clock the next morning. I felt strong, and every one of my physical senses was heightened in a way you can't under- stand unless you've been there.

Groupies And Junkies
I became the Pied Piper. Wherever I went, people followed. All day long I'd get calls from people wantin' to know where I was gonna be that night. At first I thought it was because people liked to be with me, but it didn't take me long to realize that they knew I'd be partyin' at the end of the night and they wanted to get in on the free booze and coke.

I had groupies — both men and women — all around me. I could easily blow $2,000 in a couple of days, in my arm or up my nose and my friends' noses. It was more than that some weeks. Toward the end, my overhead was gettin' so high I get a nosebleed just thinkin' about it.

Everybody Wanted a Piece Of The Action
No matter what you're into, if you're really successful there'll always be plenty of people who want to be your friend.

This is true whether you're in a legal business or illegal business. There'll always be people who hang around wantin' somethin' from you.

Every day somebody begged me for money. I had people callin' me all the time wantin' cash for this project or that one. Five thousand dollars to get into a lumber business or ten thousand dollars to buy some kind of franchise. It was ridiculous. I finally got to the point where I didn't know if they liked me, or just what they thought I could give them. Everybody had their hands out — my brother, most of my old friends. I didn't know who was actually my friend. As long as I was goin' to the bar and buyin' everybody drinks all night and handin' out blow — *everybody* was my buddy.

Overestimating Myself And Underestimating The Lady
At the end I was like every other sucker who thinks he can keep that White Lady under control.

I mean, she had my nose wide open — you could've driven a Mack truck through it. There were mornings I'd wake up and feel like an eight ball was caked inside my nose from the night before. Eventually I stopped snorting and went to mainlining and free-basing.

I was high all the time and sufferin' from drug-induced paranoia. I was ridin' a high-flyin' emotional roller coaster that never came to a stop. Some nights I'd drink a quart of whiskey, shoot a quarter ounce of coke, and eat about 10 Valium. I did the Valium just to get some sleep.

Other nights I might eat 20 Quaaludes and Valium, washin' it all down with a quart of whiskey. The only time I didn't get high was Saturday night and Sunday. It's a wonder I'm alive and that I have any brain cells left. I'm not kiddin' you. I lived like

Groupies, Lawyers and Junkies

that for about two years. My habit had finally caught up with me. I totally lost my edge and my desire to live. I had finally found out what all those other suckers already knew — that White Girl ain't no Lady!

I started breakin' all my own rules — takin' stupid chances. I got careless and lazy. The truth is, I just didn't care any more — I was too busy chasin' the Lady, and a memory of the feelin' she first gave me. Nothin' else mattered.

Kasha and Me — The Beginning Of My End

The first night Kasha and I were together was the beginning of my fall. A lot of dangerous, stupid things happened that year on my way down. This particular night, after makin' my deliveries, I went to an after-hours joint to look for Richie.

I had to be on a suicide mission because I'd left a quarter pound of cocaine sittin' on the dashboard of my car. When I arrived Richie and his friends Goldie and Kasha were just comin' out, so I pulled up to talk to them.

You guessed it. A few minutes later the cops drove up and shined their light in my car. Well, there was no way they could miss seein' my bag of coke. Richie went to one side of the cop car, and Goldie went to the other side, and Kasha jumped into the car with me and said, "Ron, get out of here, now!"

I found out later that if the cops had tried to get out of their car, Richie and Goldie were gonna do 'em right there.

Anyway, Kasha and I took off in my Trans Am and went to her place. That was the beginning of my relationship with her. I remember askin' myself the next morning what was I thinkin'? I'd been so stupid!

I'd gotten careless because I didn't give a crap about life. I thought, here I am with more money than I know what to do with, and I don't even care if I live or die. I didn't care about myself, my marriage, or my kids. This was the first time I had done a little bit of soul searching — the first time I admitted to myself that there really was somethin' wrong with my life. But I didn't care enough to do anything about it.

Kasha and I were together for about a year. She was my dream girl. She was beautiful, brilliant, and tough. She was a hot blonde, absolutely stunning to look at, but she wasn't a groupie. She was my business partner. She'd had some big acid labs in California and had done some work with the Hell's Angels.

We did a lot of gigs together. That was one crazy year. Once, on a delivery run to Madison, Wisconsin, the cops pulled us over. I had two or three kilos of coke in the trunk of my car and I was tore up. In fact, I was so drunk I couldn't walk. I was carryin' my 44, which had a hair trigger. I mean, all you'd have to do was *touch* the trigger and it would go off. When the cops pulled us over, I tossed it over on Kasha's lap. She had a fit.

The cops walked up and asked me to step out of the car, but I told them, "I can't, I'm too messed up." This would never happen today, but they made Kasha drive the car and let us go. If they'd bothered to look in my trunk, they would've had me with $300,000 worth of cocaine and pot and other drugs. I was one lucky mother that day.

This was just one more stupid incident which should have told me that my time was runnin' out. By this time any idea I might ever have had about the romance of dealin' dope was long gone. Strung out emotionally, mentally and physically, I was sick of the b.s. and tired of the game.

I didn't know it then, but it wouldn't be long before everything in my life would be turned upside down.

PART THREE:

How To Be
A Successful
Criminal

How To Be A Successful Criminal
The Real Deal On Crime, Drugs, and Easy Money

CHAPTER 7

Outside the System, Outside the Law

What It Takes To Be A Success

Hey Buddy! I know what you're thinkin': "The name of this book is How To Be a Successful Criminal, and I haven't read anything yet that tells me what I was lookin' for when I picked this sucker up."

So stop whinin' and keep readin'! The title of this book ain't no gimmick.

There's More To It Than You Think
When I say dope dealer, what's the first thing that pops into your mind? From where you stand, I'm sure it looks like one big party. If I were to ask you, "What does a drug dealer do?" you'd probably tell me that he drives a cool ride, parties, makes a lot of easy money, and has all the women and dope he wants: He's the Man! And you'd be partly right.

But what about the rest of it? The parts you don't see; the things that go on behind the scenes that keep the guy alive and successful out on the street. Most people think "easy money," because it looks easy from the outside, but once you see it from the inside, you find out it's very different. Believe me, it's not as simple as you think.

Do you have what it takes? You better have these skills or work with guys who have them if you expect to be successful.

To Be A Successful Criminal It Takes:

Ability to take risks	Perseverance
Desire	Planning
Organizational skill	Management skill
Marketing skill	Confident decision maker
Goal setting	Intuitive/observant
Product/Market knowledge	Ability to manage money
Leadership skill	Motivational skill
Common sense	Networking skill
Verbal skill	Discernment
Competitive attitude	Patience
Ability to problem solve	Salesmanship
Flexibility	People skill
Self-motivated	Good listening skills

One of the things I see happenin' across the country is that there's a lot of nickel and dime dudes out there, and most of 'em will never amount to much because they do so little organizing or planning.

Most of the people I knew who were into dope dealin' — and I knew people from all over the US — were not very good at it. They weren't businessmen, they were dabblers and eventually they either quit, got busted, or got killed.

Startin' A Business

Bottom line in any business — you gotta think through on what you're doin', and the risks you're willing to take. Do you know:

- What your goals are?
- How long you want to stay in business?
- How much money you want to make?
- If a deal goes bad, are you gonna get out, or hang in there to play another day?
- Do you put money away for a bad day? You gotta expect the unexpected.
- When are you willin' to quit the business?
- What are you willin' to give up, or lose? (Family, friends, relationships — 'cuz you will, you can count on it.)
- What kind of trainin' do you need? Who's gonna teach you the business?

Money — The Name Of The Game

Whether you're flippin' dope or runnin' a legitimate business, if you wanna stay on top of your game, you'll need money for two things: a good lawyer and the best deals on high-quality merchandise. Make sure to plan ahead.

Save Your Money And It'll Save You

It doesn't matter whether you're in a legal or illegal business, the more money you have, the more money you'll have the ability to make.

Most people, when they're flippin' dope, never think of savin' money. It goes up their nose or in their arm. Even though they're makin' more money than they can consume, they usually blow the rest on gamblin' and playin' the big shot.

Some guys spend every dime on women, cars, partyin', and b.s. It never enters their minds to save money for a lawyer, even though they know their butt belongs to the judge if they don't have money for a high-priced attorney.

Other People's Money —
Payin' Cash vs. Frontin'

Get this straight. *Nobody ever just gives you credit.* No matter what you buy on credit, it's gonna cost a whole lot more than if you paid cash. Depending on what you're buyin', you can pay as much as two to three times the original purchase price just for the credit.

If somethin' goes wrong with a deal, you could end up owing the person the rest of your life — if you still have a life when it's over.

Specialize — What's Your Product Of Choice?

No matter what kind of business you're in, it's not a good idea to spread yourself too thin. It's much easier to be successful if you pick one or two products and specialize. If you wanna reach your market, you'll have more luck using a narrow scope than the shotgun approach.

You don't go to a Chinese restaurant to buy a pizza. Even if the Chinese restaurant sold pizza, you wouldn't order it from them. You'd order Chinese food from the Chinese restaurant and get your pizza from Pizza Hut, 'cuz you know that's their specialty and it would be the best you could get.

Findin' Sources For Quality Product

Most of the time you look for the best price and the hottest product. This is where it pays to have a good network of reliable contacts. Once you've located the right source, take whatever time is necessary to develop a good relationship. Good relationships can sometimes make the difference between gettin' a good deal or a better deal.

I'd rather pay extra and get better quality. Remember: "You get what you pay for" is more than just a catchy old sayin' — it's the truth. No matter what you're buyin' or what business you're in — if you want quality, you gotta be prepared to pay quality prices.

Makin' The Deal

Always plan, and anticipate possible hang-ups. Be prepared. Go for a win/win situation where both parties benefit from the deal. This can save you from havin' problems later on.

Transportin' The Product

There's lots of different jobs in the dope business, and each one comes with its own risks. Movin' merchandise from point A to point B can become a nightmare even when you anticipate and plan for potential problems.

You have to know how and when to make the transaction. Choose the best carriers and routes. Know when to blow off the deal. Remember, if any deal sounds too good to be true, it usually is.

Only One Thing More Dangerous
Than Selling Drugs — Keepin' Them Around

Organize, organize, organize! My rule was to get rid of all my inventory in as short a time as possible. I never liked to keep anything more than a week. No matter what business you're in, you can't afford to sit on product.

Is This a Job You'd Want?

HELP WANTED:
Tough, young kids, willing to risk everything. Opportunity to work your way through the ranks of this high-paying business — if you survive. Must have good survival instincts and be able to keep your eyes open and your mouth shut. Ability to follow orders is critical. Willingness to lose your freedom or life for the sake of the business, while adult employer goes free, is expected. Willingness to blow away competition or hit some deadbeat, a must. Those interested in working in street sales must be able to think quickly on your feet and be good at math. Must be able to keep cool under fire. Must be one bad mother___, or at least able to convince people that you are. Must be willing to lose all trust in everybody and never feel free again.

I know you wouldn't go into the dope business by answerin' an ad. But let's get real, it's important for you to know what you're really gettin' into.

Skills Needed To Be A Successful Dope Dealer

<u>Task</u>	<u>Skills needed</u>
Able to put together a large working army.	Motivation. Ability to handle details. Psychological skills. Well-organized.
Slick enough to get people to do what you want them to do, when you want them to do it — no matter what.	Leadership skills. Psychological skills. Management abilities.
Willing to blow away anybody who crosses you.	Ability to make hard decisions. Ability to ignore conscience.
Willing to lose your life and/or freedom for the sake of money.	Greed.
Willing to work 80-90 hours/week or more.	Dedication. Obsessiveness. Workaholism.
Know how to convince others that you have the best stuff or that you're the baddest mother — in town.	Verbal skills. Creativity. Salesmanship. Ability to act as enforcer.
Able to read people and circumstances and use them to personal advantage.	Good observation skills. Coldheartedness. Intuition.
Willing to blow off a deal in a heartbeat if things don't look or feel right.	Confidence. Flexibility. Patience. Caution. Ability to make decisions.

Task	Skills needed
Can see what needs to be done and does it. Don't need a gun at your head to get things done right.	Motivation.
Know what's hot right now— who's buyin', where, and for what price.	Up-to-date market knowledge. Good listening skills. Good observation skills. Competitiveness.
Know how to make bad dope look good, how to cut, and how to make rock. Able to recognize quality.	Product knowledge. Working knowledge of chemistry. Lab skills.
Know how to create a demand for your service or product.	Salesmanship. Public relations skills. Marketing skills.
Able to make quick decisions under less than ideal conditions.	Confidence. Good decision maker.

Think About It

- *There's no such thing as "easy money". It don't matter what kind of business you're in, it takes preparation, and experience, before you're gonna make any real money.*
- *Instead of knowin' that money's just a tool that helps us have the kind of life we dream of, we get stuck thinkin' money is the dream.*
- *Dealin' dope is not as easy as you think.*
- *Know what you're riskin'.*
- *The more money you have, the more money you'll be able to make.*
- *Nobody ever just gives you credit.*

CHAPTER 8

Outside the System, Outside the Law

The Easy Money Scam

There's a Sucker Born Every Minute

Nobody likes to think that they can be scammed, and nobody wants to think of themselves as a sucker. I know I don't.

But I fell into one of the biggest scams out there — the dope business. I was sucked in by the excitement and a promise of fast, easy money. I told myself it would be dynamite to have a nice home and spend more time with my family.

This is the game where so many of us get conned into thinkin' that there's a quick, easy way to get our share of the good life. We get lulled into believin' that the glamorous, romantic criminal life holds the answers to all of our problems. But we never think about what it's gonna cost us.

We're already losin' before we realize that we should've read the small print at the bottom of the page before we signed up. You see, this ain't no game; it's for keeps. Because of the dope business in this country we're losin' our families, our freedom, and the pride and safety we once had in our communities. Somebody else is makin' big bucks, but you and I are losin' our lives.

Mules and runners make a lot of money in a short amount of time, but they're highly expendable. They're the throwaways of the game. Within a few short months they're usually either busted or dead. But it doesn't matter, because there are a hundred more where they come from. That's why they make the big money. Nobody at the top wants to take the kind of risks these people take.

Yeah, a lot of money went through my hands, but I lost my pride, my family, my friends, and my self-respect before I wised up and got out of the business.

The real tragedy is that when I stopped playin' the game, there was a waitin' line of hundreds standin' by to take my place. There's never a shortage of suckers. There's a new one born every minute. The thing is, you don't have to be one of 'em.

Bottom Line —
There's No Such Thing As "Easy Money"
If you watch much television, it's easy to grow up believin' that money is the answer to all of life's problems — the more money you have, the cooler you'll be; the more money you have, the happier you'll be; the more money you have, the more perfect life becomes.

Instead of knowin' that money's just a tool we have to help us have the kind of life we dream of havin', we get stuck thinkin' that money *is* the dream — that the easiest and fastest way to make money is the smartest.

All we end up thinkin' about is how to get as much as we can, as fast as we can. It doesn't matter how we get it or who we have to hurt in the process — just so there's plenty of it.

I spend a lot of time talkin' to young guys in schools and jails, and what they think they want is to connect with somebody who'll tell them how to do the perfect crime. They wanna know the best way to make lots of fast, easy money. And I'm gonna tell you what I tell them: *there's no such thing as easy money.* It doesn't matter what kind of business you're in, it takes experience, preparation, and a lot of study and time before you're gonna make money.

The drug business is just like any other business. You don't get rich overnight. It takes years of payin' your dues and hard work to make real money. You might make a little bit of money at first, but the only thing easy about it will be how easy it is to lose your self-respect, your family, your freedom, or your life in the process.

Think About It

- *The dope business is nothin' but an easy money scam.*
- *There's never a shortage of suckers. There's a new one born every minute.*
- *Bottom line — there's no such thing as easy money.*

CHAPTER 9

Who's Bein' Ripped Off?

Fences — You Do The Work, They Take The Money

Ever heard the word fence? Fences exist because guys like you don't realize you can't return stolen goods for credit at WalMart. Guess how much, if anything, you'll get for that $200 CD player. How about $10? Guess who makes all the money? I can tell you that it's not the guy out there puttin' his butt on the line. It's that geek who owns the local legal fence: The Quick Pawn, that's who.

You take all the risks, and he gives you 10 cents on the dollar, if you're lucky. He turns around and sells your merchandise at a very nice profit. Then one day the cops get a tip that this jerk is sellin' stolen property and they walk in to investigate. Mr. Fence, bein' the upstandin' citizen that he is, acts shocked, and cooperates your butt into jail. You get time, while he gets to keep his money, his business, and his good name.

There's no point cryin'. That's just the way it is. If you aren't the fence, you gotta know a good one. It's called supply and demand. You gotta know your market, and you gotta have a plan.

Actually, this is a dumb way of makin' money, unless you're gonna handle big lots, and even then there's not a whole lot of money to be made.

And you know what? Your chance of gettin' caught for theft and larceny, or burglary is higher than you think! The FBI recently reported:

- 391,950 kids, all 17 years old or younger, were arrested for theft and larceny in 1993

- 43,340 kids, all 17 years old or younger, were arrested for robbery

I don't know about you, but this tells me two things: 1) There are a lotta you out there tryin' to get over; and 2) You're not doin' a very good job of it.

Think About It

- *Some smart somebody figured out that the average inmate convicted of burglary is servin' hard time for chump change. If he'd worked for minimum wage for the number of years he served, he could've bought more than he ever stole.*

CHAPTER 10

Your Chances Of Becoming A Successful Criminal

No Such Thing As a Successful Criminal

According to the cops, there's no such thing as a successful criminal. They say that if you choose to live outside the law, you choose to lose. And you know what? If you look at the numbers, they're right!

The truth is nobody ever really gets away with it. For a few years it may seem like they're really gettin' over, but in the end they all wind up pretty much the same.

Even many of the guys who could be at the top of any business they choose wind up dead or spendin' the best years of their lives in jail. I'm not talkin' about pretenders and wannabes. I'm talkin' about the cream of the crop. The genius minds who've created and led some of the top criminal enterprises in the world. The Original Gangsters.

They're ruthless, self-motivated, self-confident, persistent planners, and risk takers. They're good at sellin' themselves and their ideas. They know how to use language, personal appearance, power, and style to create their own unique image of success.

I'm talkin' about guys like Al Capone, John Gotti, and Sammy Gravano; Harry "Taco" Bowman, international leader of the Outlaw's Motorcycle Club; Larry Hoover, charismatic leader of the Gangster Disciples; Tookie Williams, leader of the Crips; Jeff Forte, powerful leader of El Rukns (Black "P." Stone Nation); and Sonny "Gangster" Jackson, member of the original Circle of 21 of the Black "P." Stone Nation.

What if *you* started a gang like the Bloods, Gangster Disciples, Crips, or Hell's Angels? Imagine for a minute what it must have been like to be one of these powerful leaders. Picture yourself with their power, all the money you can spend, and women crawlin' all over themselves to be with you. Can you see yourself drivin' around in your new ride?

How much gold would you be wearin' around your neck? How much would you have spent on your clothes? How many guns would you be carryin', and how many bodyguards would you be payin'? How many Mercedes and Jaguars would you own? How many houses would you own, and in which states would they be located? How many vacations do you think you'd be goin' on, and in which countries?

Now think about the opposite for a minute. Do you think these dreams ever really come true?

Almost Every Gang Leader Ends Up Dead Or In Jail Without Parole
When their home is a 6x8 foot jail cell for 10, 20, or up to 150 years, how many women do you think they get? Who's sleepin' with their wives? Who's raisin' their kids? Who's drivin' their Mercedes now? There's only so much soap and toothpaste they can buy with all that money while they're in the joint.

Where Are They Today?

Each of these powerful leaders had their 15 minutes of glory.
But look where they are today.

Larry Hoover Leader of Gangster Disciples	Servin' life without possibility of parole at super-max USP in Florence, Colorado*.
John Gotti Godfather, Gambino Crime Family	Servin' life without parole in a 6' x 8' cell at the super-max USP in Florence, Colorado*.
Jeff Forte Black "P." Stone Nation	Servin' 167 years without parole in the USP at Marion, Illinois*. Can hardly remember what it was like to drive a car.
Al Capone Most powerful man in Chicago for 20 years.	Spent seven years in Alcatraz, where he lost his power and his rep. He died alone of syphilis at age 47.
Sammy Gravano Underboss, Gambino Crime Family	Turned federal witness. Gravano lost his family, his name, his identity, his money, and his reputation, and is out there on his own in his early 50's tryin' to make a new life for himself.
Harry "Taco" Bowman International Leader of the Outlaws Motorcycle Club	Has gone underground in order to evade capture. On the FBI's Ten Most Wanted Fugitive List. The government has placed a $50,000 bounty on his head. Wanted dead or alive.
Stanley "Tookie" Williams One of the founders of the Crips	Currently on death row, San Quentin, California. Other co-founder is dead.

*The United States Penitentiaries (USP) at Marion, Illinois and Florence, Colorado are Control Unit Prisons. They operate under a "super-maximum security regime. They may differ in some minor details, but are similar in the following:

1. Prisoners are kept in solitary confinement in 6x8 foot cubicles for 22-23 hours per day. They eat alone in their cells, exercise alone, and are never allowed contact with other inmates. No work opportunities and no religious services.

2. Lockdown conditions are permanent, according to official prison policy.

3. Conditions are officially justified not as punishment for prisoners, but as administrative measures. There are no rules which govern administrative measures; therefore prisoners are denied due process, and prison officials can incarcerate ANY prisoner in a control unit for as long as they choose, without having to give a reason.

If these brilliant, creative geniuses weren't able to keep from losin' everything they had, what makes you think you can?

Well, I'm here to tell you, there's no way you can become a successful criminal. You can't succeed workin' outside the system, and outside the law. I've never met anybody who hasn't lost big when they tried to play the game. If you're lucky, you'll only lose your dignity, your pride, your self-esteem, your sanity, your wife or partner, your family and friends. If you're one of the unlucky ones, you'll end up losin' your freedom or your life.

You won't know who to trust. It's likely that you'll become suicidal. You'll be lookin' over your shoulder when the problem is probably starin' you in your face — right in front of you. You'll become mean, desperate, and out of control. Your greatest fears will come true, and you'll wind up paranoid, empty, and alone.

Look, I've never met anybody who wants to be a true criminal. A true criminal is a person shunned by the world, respected by no one, hated by many, ignored by most, and treated only somewhat humanely when he's locked up.

We all want to be the kind of criminal we see on television.
You know, the one's makin' money, shootin' guns, drivin' fast
cars. The ones who are respected, feared, adored, and idolized — the ones who run the show.

The truth is, criminals spend more time in jail than they do in
fast cars. They end up alone and in juvenile detention, prison,
or an early grave.

Your chances of becomin' successful in the crime business is *a*
big fat zero, because the odds are all against you. Crime is a
losin' game. There are no real winners, and there's no such
thing as easy money.

Think About It

- *There's no such thing as a successful criminal. Even*
  the most brilliant leaders end up dead or losin' their
  freedom.
- *Nobody wants to be a real criminal. We all want to be*
  the kind of criminal we see on television and in the
  movies.

CHAPTER 11

Truth
And
Consequences

Just For the Record

I wanna set the record straight. I would never have done business the way I see some guys doin' it today. It's bad enough when a man gets suckered into riskin' his life by the promise of fast, easy money. But it's way out of line for him to protect himself by hidin' behind some young kid while he's doin' it. What kind of man hides behind kids?

Sure, it's cheap protection for the guy runnin' the show to sacrifice your little behind to protect his own. But what's really in it for you?

Butt Wipes

You're bein' manipulated to take the fall for these mothers. These dudes are payin' you to be their mules, lookouts, and runners. You're broke; this looks like easy money, and you'll do anything to be accepted and look cool.

But I have a news flash: *they're usin' you like butt wipes.* In fact, a friend of mine calls you the Charmin Toilet Paper Detail:

an easy way for them to keep *their* butts clean. You're disposable, and there's always more where you came from. They use you until you're all used up, and then they go on to the next butt wipe.

These guys are gettin' you kids to risk your lives for them by tellin' you that the legal system is easier on you. This may have been true a few years ago, but it ain't true anymore. And now, they've got armies of you out there killin' one another while they sit back rakin' in the money. What's up with that?

Runnin' To Catch The Money Train

The deal is, you kids are chasin' the money train, and for a while you're makin' more money than you ever dreamed possible. Where else is a 12- or 13-year-old gonna get $1000 a week? You don't care about bein' busted. You're hooked on the money. Who wouldn't be? In fact, if I was 12 or 13 and on the streets I'd probably be doin' the same thing. At your age, I wasn't any smarter than you are.

All I have to say is, man, you have a choice. You can educate yourself and make somethin' of your life, or you can choose the dope business. But just know that if you do, you'll probably be in it the rest of your life. And you'll be snortin' or shootin' the stuff just like everybody else. Human beings weren't created to deal with the kind of violence and stress you'll be under.

The money becomes such a habit that even a couple trips to the joint can't keep you from goin' back for more. It's a dead man's road. You'll end up in a stone cold grave — or, if you're one of the lucky ones, you'll become a three-time loser and the judge will put you in the joint as an habitual criminal. If that happens, there's a good chance you'll get to stay there the rest of your life.

Where's The Real Money Goin'?

When you're young, crime can look like a shortcut to the good life: money, power, women, and prestige. It's easy to get caught up in the deadly game bein' played out across the country. Criminal gangs aren't just a big city thing. There's hardly a town anywhere that doesn't have a problem with gang graffiti, drugs, and violence. What the hippie culture was to kids in the 60's, the subculture of the gangster gang has become to kids in the 90's.

I'm not judgin' this, I'm simply makin' an observation. And let's face it, it's not just the gangsters who're makin' money. The movie, music, clothing, and fashion industries all get their cuts as they make this subculture the standard for *cool*.

Can't Touch Me

I know you think bad things only happen to other people — that you're smart and can take care of yourself. *You're* not gonna kill or get killed by anybody, get busted, or spend the rest of your life in the joint like some tired old loser. *You're* not gonna live your life in a wheelchair, crippled from a gunshot wound. These things happen to your cousin, your neighbor, or your brother. They don't ever happen to you.

Hey, at your age you're supposed to think that way. This ability is what makes young people such dreamers and risk-takers. It allows you to look at a seemingly impossible task, problem, or situation and ask, "Who says it's impossible?"

Let's face it, if the teenagers of early America hadn't believed they could defeat Europe's most powerful military force, we'd still be singin' England's "God Save the Queen."

Just don't let this blind you to the realities of life. Be informed and think things through, so that whatever path you choose, you won't be one of the whiners cryin', "I wish I'd known then what I know now!" I'm givin' you the opportunity to be in the know right *now*. That's what this book is all about.

Who You're Up Against

This is the deal: if you're into any type of illegal business in this country, you've got one of the largest armies of law enforcement agencies in the world dedicated to your failure. *The only reason they exist is to keep you from bein' successful.*

This army is made up of local and state law enforcement agencies, the Drug Enforcement Agency (DEA), the Federal Bureau of Investigation (FBI), the Alcohol, Firearms and Tobacco Agency (AFT), and the Internal Revenue Service (IRS) — to name only a few. They have a multi-billion dollar budget to spend on quality manpower and 21st century technology, all used for one purpose — to bring you down!

Their success is based on your failure. These organizations dedicate themselves to learnin' everything they can about crime and criminals. They know more about you than you want to know about yourself. You may experience short-term success, but man, in the long run, the odds are against you.

Listen, if you're repeatedly gettin' over on the cops, they take it personally. Don't think that you can be successfully involved in any heavy-duty business over a long period of time without them puttin' constant pressure on you to bring you down. In fact, the bigger you get, and the more invincible you think you are, the more vulnerable you actually become. *They can get anybody if they want to;* just ask Manuel Noriega or the boys from the Colombian drug cartels.

Wake up! You don't have to just worry about the competition, wiretaps, jealous punks, and snitches. If you're big enough, and the cops want to know what you're up to, they've got eavesdroppin' technology that would make you swear that your old lady's a snitch. They have the ability to pick up on you from fifty miles away, and "make" everything that you say or do, just as though they were in the same room with you. Understand one thing: *there's not another business you could be in where you will experience this kind of pressure to fail.*

What You're Up Against
Even though the overall crime rate is decreasing, teenage violent crime in the United States is about to explode. Violent crimes committed by adults have declined, but the violent crimes committed by kids between the ages of 12 and 17 have skyrocketed.

Get this:
- Between 1984 and 1993, the teen murder rate increased by 169%.
- In 1992, 17-year-olds were five times more likely to be arrested for homicide than 33-year-olds. That year, minors killed over 3,400 people.
- Juvenile assault with a deadly weapon rose from 73,987 in 1982 to143,368 in 1992.
- FBI statistics claim that 40% of *all crimes* committed in the United States are by young people under the age of 25, and that 30% of *all violent crimes* are committed by kids under the age of 21.

So does it surprise you that a couple of years later, the 1994 Crime Bill provided for 100,000 new officers on the street, authorized $7 billion for development of new crime prevention programs, and allowed kids *13 years old* who've been charged with violent crimes (murder, armed robbery, rape, etc.) to be *treated as adults*? You heard me, I said 13-year-olds, chump!

Anti-Gang And Youth Violence Act Of 1997: Instead Of Fresh Meat, Now You're Dead Meat
In 1997, as a part of the Senate's full-scale assault on juvenile crime, Senator Leahy introduced the Anti-Gang and Youth Violence Act of 1997. The Act is part of the Federal Government's

strategy to *"break the back of violent gangs and reduce youth violence."*

Under the authority of this Act, federal prosecutors will be able to start a major crackdown. By usin' the powerful Racketeering Influenced and Corrupt Organization (RICO) statute, they plan to more than double federal prosecutions of violent gangs.

The Anti-Gang and Youth Violence Act of 1997 will make it a federal offense for juvenile gang members to commit the following "serious crimes": criminal homicide, forcible rape or other sex offenses punishable as felonies, hate crimes, mayhem, kidnapping, aggravated assault, robbery, larceny or theft punishable as a felony, motor vehicle theft, burglary or breaking and entering, extortion accompanied by threats of violence, drug trafficking, firearms violations, or felony arson. Gang members and other violent juveniles arrested for such offenses will be tried and sentenced as adults.

The Death Penalty:
It Really Cuts Down Your Time In the Joint
Here's another news flash for you! Durin' the past eight years, the U.S. has executed more juvenile offenders than any other country.

In the United States today:

- Thirty-eight states use the death penalty.
- Only thirteen of these states have set the minimum age for execution at 18.
- Four states have set the minimum age at 17.
- Twenty-one states have set their minimum age for execution at 16 or have no minimum age at all.
- Between 1973 and 1993, 121 kids under the age of 18 received the death penalty.
- Thirteen of these kids were 15 years old.
- Twenty-four of the 121 were 16 years old.
- Seventy were 17 years old.
- So far nine of these juvenile offenders have been executed, six during the past eight years.

Are you gettin' the message? These people mean business. The American public is fed up. They don't care how victimized you've been, they don't care how poor and underprivileged you are! That sad song just ain't cuttin' it in the 90's like it did in the 60's, 70's, and 80's. John and Jane Q. Public have sent a strong message to the state and federal governments telling them they want juvenile crime and violence stopped.

There's not a city in America today that isn't concerned about youth crime and violence. Wake up, man! The heat's bein' turned up, and if you're not careful, you're gonna get burned. The streets are only gonna get hotter.

There are only six countries in the world where it's legal to execute someone who committed a crime before their 18th birthday: Iran, Pakistan, Nigeria, Saudi Arabia, Yemen and the United States. All of these countries, except the U.S., have an international reputation for severe human-rights violations. Russia and China have outlawed the execution of juveniles. But the U.S. has passed laws which make it *easier* to use the death penalty against kids.

Think About It

- *If you're breakin' the law in this country, you've got one of the largest armies of law enforcement agencies in the world dedicated to your failure. The only reason they exist is to keep you from bein' successful. There's not another business you could be in where you'll experience this kind of pressure to fail.*
- *Last year the federal government launched a full-scale assault to break the back of violent gangs and reduce youth violence. Durin' the past eight years, the U.S. has executed more juvenile offenders than any other country in the world.*

CHAPTER 12

New Rules For Dealin' Dope: Rule One — You're Screwed Rule Two — See Rule One

Gettin' convicted for drug sales is a whole lot easier than it used to be. Today you don't have to be in possession of large amounts of dope to be charged and convicted of sales. In fact, in some states, you don't have to be in possession of anything but a beeper, a "balance sheet," and have more than $100 in your pocket.

Drug trafficking and sales receive much heavier penalties than they did a few years ago. Some first-time juvenile offenders still receive lighter sentences than adults because the courts want to give kids an opportunity to get straight. But if you continue in the life, you'll be tried as an adult. That means you'll wind up with a longer sentence and be sent to a state juvenile facility or adult penitentiary.

If you've been convicted of flippin' dope more than once and you're caught with a gun, you can now get as much as 15 years under the Armed Career Criminal Act. In the past this law was used against adult career criminals. Today it can be used against kids.

I'm gonna say it again: you can't hide behind your age any more. If you commit a serious crime, then in many cases, you're gonna be tried and sentenced as an adult. Check this out:

Federal Trafficking Penalties as of January 1996	
Drug	Quantity
Methamphetamine	10-99 gm pure or 100-999 gm mixture
Heroin	100-999 gm mixture
Cocaine	500-4,999 gm mixture
Cocaine Base	5-49 gm mixture
PCP	10-99 gm pure or 100-999 gm mixture
LSD, Peyote	1-9 gm mixture
1st Offense*	2nd Offense*
Not less than 5 yrs. Not more than 40 yrs.	Not less than 10 yrs. Not more than life.
If death or serious injury, not less than 20 yrs., or more than life.	If death or serious injury, not less than life.
Fine not more than $2 million individual, $5 million other than individual.	Fine not more than $4 million individual, $10 million other than individual.

* These penalties apply to all substances listed above. Increased quantities bring increased penalties.

Federal Trafficking Penalties For Marijuana as of January 1996

Drug	Quantity	1st Offense	2nd Offense
Marijuana	1,000 kg or more mixture; or 1,000 or more plants	Not less than 10 yrs., not more than life. If death or serious injury, not less than 20 yrs., not more than life. Fine not more than $4 million individual, $10 million other.	Not less than 20 yrs . Not more than life. If death or serious injury, not more than life. Fine not more than $8 million individual $20 million other.
Marijuana	100-999 kg mixture; or 100-999 plants	Not less than 5 yrs., not more than 40 yrs. If death or serious injury, not less than 20 yrs., not more than life. Fine not more than $2 million individual, $5 million other.	Not less than 10 yrs. not more than life. If death or serious injury not more than life. Fine not more than $4 million individual $10 million other.
Marijuana	50-99 kg mixture; or 50-99 plants	Not more than 20 yrs. If death or serious injury, not less than 20 yrs., not more than life. Fine $1 million individual, $5 million other.	Not more than 30 yrs. If death or serious not more than life. Fine $2 million individual, $10 million other.
Marijuana	Less than 50 kg mixture	Not more than 5 yrs. Fine not more than $250,000 individual, $1 million other.	Not more than 10 yrs. Fine $500,000 individual, $2 million other.
Hashish	10 kg or more	Not more than 5 yrs. Fine not more than $250,000 individual, $1 million other.	Not more than 10 yrs. Fine $500,000 individual, $2 million other.
Hashish oil	1 kg or more	Not more than 5 yrs. Fine not more than $250,000 individual, $1 million other.	Not more than 10 Fine $500,000 individual, $2 million other.

New Rules For Dealin' Dope: Rule One, You're Screwed — Rule Two, See Rule One

---

Think About It

- *Bein' convicted of flippin' dope is a whole lot easier than it used to be.*
- *Convictions for trafficking and sales receive heavier penalties than in the past.*
- *If you do the crime, expect to do the time.*

CHAPTER 13

Why Do Ya Think They Call It Dope?

At some point in the game you'll more than likely get strung out on drugs because your body and mind weren't created to take the kind of stress that comes with a criminal lifestyle. And here's the catch: a true professional would never be high or drunk while doin' a job. They know how risky it is and how much easier it is to blow it if somethin' goes wrong.

If you're spendin' most of your time and energy workin' outside the system and outside the law, then there's somethin' you oughtta know.

Close to 90% of the people sittin' in jail admit that they either have a drug or alcohol problem or were under the influence of drugs or alcohol at the time of their arrest. Most inmates claim that they wouldn't have even committed the crime they were arrested for if it hadn't been for the fact that they were high, or needin' to buy their next fix so they could get high.

Do you know how stupid it is when you drink or use dope before you do a crime? When you're high your reflexes diminish, you get a false sense of well being, and an exaggerated sense of power. You might feel like drugs or alcohol make you sharper, but nothin' is further from the truth. In fact, in most cases if you're thinkin' straight, you'll have enough sense not to do the job at all.

Did ya hear about the guy who was so messed up that he stopped in the bank to count the money he had just robbed from one of the tellers? There are so many idiots out there that whole books are bein' written about criminals and the stupid things they do.

If You Don't Remember Anything Else, Remember This:

When you get high before a job, there's a greater risk for things to get out of control. If you're messed up on alcohol or drugs, your greatest strength will become your greatest weakness. What otherwise might have led to your success now trips you up and works against you.

It's like this: if you're a risk taker, you're gonna get reckless and take a bad fall. You're not takin' a risk anymore — you're commitin' suicide.

Wake up! If you've got a drug or alcohol problem, get rid of it. Clean up your act and stop playin' the victim. 'Cuz guess what, brother, the cops don't get high before they set out to get you. Their judgment and vision aren't clouded or distorted by chemicals. So why put yourself at such a disadvantage? Think about it.

No professional person can afford to be drunk or high on the job. If the head teller of a bank was drunk or high at work and gave you $100,000 instead of $1,000, how long do you think he'd be the head teller?

When you're messed up you lose your ability to stay on top of everything. Your intuition gets blurred, you get cocky, and you begin to over estimate yourself and underestimate everybody else. And brother, if you get caught in this trap, you're on your way down and out.

When you're high you don't think about the fact that you're only 20 years old and starin' at 40 years hard time because you got ticked off or paranoid and shot some fool. You won't see daylight until you're 60 years old because you got wasted and lost it.

Do Yourself a Favor

Lock yourself in a small bathroom for half a day. While you're in there, imagine that the tub is a steel cot, the big sink is a small metal one, and that there's no seat on the toilet. Now visualize one last thing: that the bathroom door is replaced by bars and there ain't no privacy.

Can you imagine what it would be like to spend the next 800 days locked up in this place? If you're lucky, that's the 2 years and 2 months you're gonna get for the first burglary you're caught doin' (most people get 5-10 years).

Look, buddy, it's hard enough to do a couple years for a burglary, but it's better than havin' to spend 7,300 days in a tiny cell for killin' somebody because you were too high to think straight.

They say alcohol and driving don't mix. Well, I gotta tell you — bein' high or drunk before doin' a crime is showin' your real I.Q.

Think About It

- *Professionals don't get high before goin' to work.*
- *Ninety percent of the people sittin' in jail admit that they either have a drug or alcohol problem or were under the influence of drugs or alcohol at the time of their arrest.*

CHAPTER 14

Doin' Time

City And County Jails

Every nightmare story you've ever heard about bein' in jail is probably true. As far as I'm concerned, doin' time in a county jail is the worst. You know when you first walk in the door that anything can happen, and anybody who tells you that they weren't scared the first time they went to jail is either lyin' or crazy.

County jail is a place where lots of violence happens — beatings, stabbings, rapes, even murders. For one thing, there are too many people in a small space. It's a proven fact that overcrowding causes an increase in stress and violence — even in rats.

And then you have the fact that everyone's thrown in together. Everybody's processed through the same jail. The most violent criminals are thrown in with everybody else, so there's no tellin' who you might end up havin' as your cellmate.

Odds are, if you're a young, fresh-lookin' kid, you're gonna have to be prepared to fight, unless you've always dreamed of

116

havin' some guy pin a Playboy centerfold to your back and call you "baby." Some guys just can't take it. It's not unusual to read about some high-school kid picked up for a DUI, or some other traffic violation, committin' suicide in a city or county jail.

State And Federal Prisons

Doin' hard time's no picnic, no matter where you do it. But man, there's nothin' in this world like the feelin' you get the first time your bus pulls into the state prison and you're greeted by every pervert and idiot in the place callin', "Hey baby, what's happenin'?" — tellin' you to get ready to party tonight.

A lot of it's a game, just to get inside your head, but there's always a couple of those boys standin' at the fence who really mean it. The truth is, if you're young and tender, you're probably gonna have sex your first night in state prison, whether you want to or not. Count on it. That's the way it is.

Not only do you have to put up with this from the other inmates, but the cops are also playin' with your head 'cuz they want you to understand what's happenin' to you and they don't want any crap out of you.

New Kid On the Block?
You've Never Been On A Block Like This

After you get off the bus, you'll walk down the lonely aisle of tears and get your little bedroll and your powdered toothpaste and toothbrush.

If you know somebody goin' in, you'll have fewer problems. But if you don't know anybody and you're walkin' in cold, it's a scary thing.

When it really gets serious is the first time they put you into the general population and you walk out onto that big yard — the new kid on the block. That's when you find out what you're really all about.

If you're lucky, somebody'll pick you up, take you under their wing, and make sure nothin' happens to you. But if you sit around runnin' your mouth about how bad you are or how smart you are or how much money you have, you're gonna wind up payin' somebody a monthly check to keep him or his friends from doin' you.

Ya Gotta Let Go Of The Street

Makin' the transition from your old street life to your new life is hard, but it has to be done. The truth is, the fewer attachments you have to the outside, the easier it'll be on you. The guys who have wives and girlfriends on the outside are more vulnerable, and more likely to get into trouble, than the guys who don't. If you're doin' hard time, it's better to keep your mind on the present, dealin' with what is, instead of wishin' for what used to be. You have to give it up — otherwise, you could become a time bomb waitin' to explode.

It's Like Bein' Dead,
Only Ya Gotta Live Through It

People always say that they'll stay in touch with you, and the first year you might hear from almost everybody. The second year you'll hear from Mom, your girlfriend, and a couple of other people. The third year it's only one friend and Mom, and the fourth year it's just Mom, and the fifth year it's just Mom, and the sixth year it's just Mom. Your friends forget about you. Outta sight, outta mind.

Keepin' Your Heart In The Street
Will Mess You Up

Besides, there's no way you can control what's happenin' on the outside. Keepin' your mind and heart in the street will eat you up inside, and get you into a load of trouble, especially if you're doin' time with the feds. 'Cuz brother, if the feds decide you're emotionally unbalanced, you're given what they call a PIN number.

Until you get that number lifted off your name, you'll never walk out the door. Your sentence stops! You get sent to a medical facility for evaluation. If they determine you're a little goofy, they send you right back to where you came from with the PIN number attached to your jacket. Every year they re-evaluate you until they think that you're better. Only then will your time start again. This is a very dangerous situation to get into, 'cuz it's a whole lot easier to get that PIN number than to get rid of it.

State prisons house criminals who've committed crimes against humanity — rape, murder, etc. — while federal inmates usually have been involved with more sophisticated crimes like coun-terfeiting, bank robbery, or dope dealing. In fact, most federal inmates today are in prison because of their involvement in the dope business. Usually, the only time you see a murderer in a federal prison is if he's Native American, a federal law enforce-ment agent, or someone who killed the President or some other top-ranking politician.

Cons Run Most Prisons

Even though cons run most prisons, and the guards are there basically to enforce the rules, federal prisons tend to be cleaner and are run more smoothly than state facilities. For one thing, state prisons house more weirdos. So naturally the odds of a young punk gettin' into some serious trouble while in a state prison are much greater than if he's in the federal system.

Don't get me wrong. No matter what they say in the press, doin' time in the federal system is no vacation at Club Med! For one thing, the federal prison system is controlled by the Depart-ment of Justice. State and local authorities have no authority over federal prisons and have no access to them. Everything that goes on within the walls of the federal prison is tightly controlled by the federal government through the Department of Justice.

Imagine Yourself In a Self-Storage Unit
"Super-Max": New Federal Control Unit Prisons

If for some reason they decide you're unfit for the general population, instead of bein' sent to the hole for a few days, authorities now have new super-max facilities they can send you to. These new maximum security prisons are run by computers, not cons. Prisoners are confined in 6'x8' individual cubicles without air conditioning, TV, or radio. Here, prison food takes on a whole new meanin'. Cons aren't given regular food, but are forced to eat nutrient-dense substances which have been ground up, mixed together and baked into loaves. Communication with other inmates is not allowed. Such severe social isolation and sensory deprivation have caused some inmates to lose their minds.

Think About It

- *Every nightmare story you've ever heard about bein' in jail is probably true.*
- *If you're doin' hard time, it's better to keep your mind on the present, dealin' with what is, instead of wishin' for what used to be.*
- *Super-max control unit prisons are run by computers, not cons.*

PART FOUR:

How To Be Successful Without Being A Criminal

CHAPTER 15

Outside The System, Inside The Law

Success On The Street Takes More Than a Beeper And a Bad Attitude

By now I hope you've figured out that anybody can pick up a one-way ticket to the morgue or the joint. But if you wanna live long and prosper on the streets, you gotta bring more than a bad attitude and a beeper. It takes organization, careful planning, and lots of hard work to stay on top of your game.

Now, if you think that you can hang with me, I wanna give you a head start to a whole new level of thinkin'. If you're willin' to give 100% to be successful, then why not invest yourself in somethin' where the odds are more in your favor? Get into somethin' that gives you a real chance of havin' a good life.

It takes the same abilities to be successful in an illegal business as it does in a legal business. Does that surprise you?

After I got out of the dope business, and started sellin' machine tools, I began to watch and listen to the guys who were the most successful salesmen. Guess what I learned — there wasn't a whole lot of difference between successfully sellin' dope and sellin' machine tools. I began to realize that most successful people have certain ways they think and act — no matter what business they're in. Here's what I mean:

Successful people —
... know how to sell themselves.
On the streets, this means knowin' how to "show up"; it's the ability to make people believe you've got your game together — bein' able to convince your competition that you're more ruthless than they are, and that they had better not mess with you; that you keep your word and are able to deliver on your threats as well as your promises. It also means bein' able to convince your customers that you have the best merchandise in town.

... aren't victims of circumstances.
This is about havin' big enough balls to live and work above the circumstance of the moment. Not bein' limited by what others do or say. Bein' willin' to go after what you want no matter what the road blocks are along the way.

... are goal oriented.
This is knowin' what you want, and how and where to go to get it. Knowin' what it will take to get you where you want to be. Being willing to take the risks and "pay the dues" that'll get you there.

... are risk takers.
Successful people are willin' to try things that haven't been done before. If you're on the streets, bein' a risk taker means puttin' your money, your freedom or life on the line. Because of this, it's real important to minimize your risks through evaluation, planning, and preparation.

... are decision makers.
This is the ability to go beyond the fear of doin' it wrong, and

not get snagged by the "what if's" in order to make difficult, quick decisions. Bein' able to "shoot from the hip" can mean the difference between success and failure — and sometimes life and death.

... have knowledge related to customers, competition, products and limitations.
This keeps successful people from overestimating themselves and underestimating everyone else. This is where you combine intuition with hard objective fact. It's called doin' your home-work.

Outside The System, Outside The Law
It's like this: a criminal works outside the system and outside the law.   He doesn't have to put up with a lot of the b.s. that comes with workin' inside the system, but he does business at great risk to his personal freedom and life.

Inside The System, Inside The Law
This just means bein' an employee, and workin' for someone else.   Let's get it straight. Whether you're makin' six figures a year or six bucks an hour, you're still workin' for The Man.

Inside The System, Outside The Law
Workin' inside the system, outside the law is what white collar criminals do. These are the guys who work the big money scams. They cross the fine line between creativity and crime, and wind up doin' lots of federal time.

Now I'm gonna tell you about some ways to decrease your risks, and increase your returns. But you'll have to be willin' to work outside the system and inside the law.

Outside The System, Inside The Law
What does that mean?

It means havin' your own business. Doin' what *you* want. Bein' an entrepreneur — someone who has the guts to organize, manage, and assume the risk of their own business. Dope dealers do this every day, but they do it outside the law.

Rules Represent The System — That's Why We Like To Break 'Em

You and I hate to live by the rules, so we make our own. This gets us into big trouble, because every society has a set of rules people agree to live by. These rules explain how to handle almost everything — from government to business to a person's life. The rules change only when most people's beliefs change. And as the rules change, the laws that reflect these rules are changed, too.

It used to be illegal for blacks and whites to use the same drinking fountains and toilets. They were required by law to attend separate schools, but today it's illegal to deny service to anyone based on race, color, creed, sex, or age.

It used to be that people got hung for stealing horses. Even though some states still have this law on their books, no one's hangin' horse thieves today. As times and people's attitudes change, many of the old laws just don't apply.

It used to be that the system and the law were about the same. But things are changin' so quickly that this isn't true any more. It's now possible to live and work outside the traditional system and not break the law.

Today there are more and more people who choose to work outside the system, but inside the law. Some of these people were a part of the system in the past, but decided that there had to be a better way of livin'. Some of them lost their jobs because of layoffs made by big businesses. But some of us have chosen to create successful lives outside a system which hadn't rewarded us in the past.

Wake up! *The world has changed.* There've always been people who lived outside the system, but people looked at them like they were either criminals or crazy. That's not true today. Every day, all kinds of people are livin' exciting, successful lives outside the mainstream system.

The Way It Was — Inside The System

For more than 200 years, a bunch of rich white men made and enforced the rules that everybody lived by. They ran the government, controlled public education, and determined how the established business world should operate. For a long time, their system was the accepted way of doin' things in this country.

I'm not sayin' this was good or bad. I'm just tellin' you how things were so that you can see what's goin' on now.

Right now we're in the middle of some very big changes — in our country and in the world. These changes have opened up all kinds of opportunities for creative thinkers like us, and I don't want you to miss out on a chance to get in on them.

It used to be that if you wanted to make a lot of money and have people look up to you, there really weren't too many legal ways to do it. Unless you were an entertainer or a star athlete, you had to go to college, get that piece of paper, and work in one of the big four: business, engineering, medicine, or law.

In other words, you had to fit into the system of the professional working class. You worked for an organization that did everything to make sure that the system continued to survive. Eventually, you became a robot and brown-nosed a lot to move up the corporate ladder.

If You Played By The Rules,
You Worked For Little Or Nothin'

And where did that leave the rest of us who didn't fit into the system, who didn't want to work for The Man in sterile little air-conditioned offices? Well, for the most part, *out of luck.* Most people scraped by in dead-end jobs they hated.

After unions lost most of their power and prestige, people had very little control over how much money they made, when they worked, or even how to do their jobs. Nobody cared what workers thought or how they felt, as long as they showed up to punch the clock. The lucky ones with seniority worked nine-to-five; the rest worked whatever shifts they could get.

A lot of people are still doin' these kinds of jobs. But I want you to understand that you have more choices than just workin' for The Man or makin' money on the street. Today smart, creative people like us make their own rules, *without* breakin' the law and endin' up in jail.

How Does All This Affect You?

It used to be that companies had people who worked for them full time to provide different services. But now they've gotten rid of a lot of those jobs, and so to get things done they have to use the services of outside people.

This means that you can make some real money without workin' for The Man, without havin' a college degree, without goin' to the joint, and without riskin' your life.

It means that if you want, you can do work for big companies without havin' to be owned by them. You can create your own job, set your own hours, and be your own boss.

It means you have choices that people didn't have before.

It means that if you're willing to put in the time, get the knowledge, training or education you need, and work as hard for yourself as you did on the street, you can write your own meal ticket. You won't have to worry about gettin' busted, ripped off, or blown away, but you'll still get the rush that comes with gettin' over.

Workin' For Yourself —
No Cops, No Judges, No Guards
What if I could tell you some ways to make an average of $50,000 a year workin' for yourself? This is nearly double the national average. Would you be interested in checking them out?

Lots Of People Not As Smart As You Are Doin' It
Hey, this is no scam! You really *don't* have to work for The Man in order to make good money. How do I know? I've done it. And according to *Entrepreneur Magazine,* there are about 14 million people out there no smarter or luckier than you and me who are out there doin' it every day. *Twenty-seven million Americans are involved in their own home businesses — 14 million do it full time and make an average of $50,000/yr. The rest do it part time.*

Yeah, I know some of these people *are* sellin' Amway, but not most of 'em. And if you think that the only way to go into business for yourself is to sign up with some network marketing business, think again. However, it might interest you to know that in this country, for the past several years, network marketing has been the number-one way people have become millionaires.

Think About It

- *Bein' a successful criminal is harder than you think.*
- *The system has changed, and so have the rules.*
- *If you're gonna give 100% to be successful, why not do somethin' where the odds are in your favor?*

CHAPTER 16

Lots Of Ways Of Doin' It

I grew up thinkin' the only thing I could ever be good at was crime. It never crossed my mind that I had what it takes to do anything else with my life. It wasn't until I was 33 years old that I finally believed there were some other things I could be good at. Hopefully I can save you some time, so it won't take you that many years.

If you're havin' a hard time believing that it takes the same skills to be successful in a legal business as an illegal business, then step outside that way of thinkin' and check this out:

If You're Good At	You Might Be A Great
• Dope dealin'	Business owner or entrepreneur Sales or sales manager
• Car theft	Auto mechanic Auto detailer Auto inspector Auto salesman

If You're Good At	You Might Be A Great
• Burglary	Locksmith Alarm systems specialist Police officer
• Extortion	Body guard Bouncer Used car salesman Insurance salesman
• Forgery	Handwriting analyst Artist Tattoo artist Commercial artist Draftsman
• Bank robbery	DEA agent Highway patrolman Airline pilot

It took me about twenty seconds to come up with these ideas, and I know some of 'em are pretty outrageous. That's why I invite you to get with some of your brothers and come up with ideas that'll work for you. I know it might sound like a drag to you. I used to hate it when somebody would try to get me to do somethin' like this. But so what? You gotta be smarter than me, so go for it.

Or What About . . .
Are you into computers? What about starting a computer repair service, or runnin' your own programming business, or designing other people's web pages? It's not that hard to turn your interests into a profitable on-line business.

Did you know that there are people who are making $45,000

a year just goin' to other people's homes and caring for their pets while they're away? This is a relatively new industry, so you wouldn't have much competition.

OK, so you're allergic to animals, but you love music and you have a great rap! Ever thought of becomin' a disc jockey? How would you like to make $50 an hour performin' at corporate gatherings, parties, and weddings?

Do people compliment you on your sense of style? Image consultants make an average of $80,000 a year helping people enhance their appearance, or teaching employees how to project their company's desired corporate image.

Would you like a business that allows you to be physically active? What about havin' your own commercial painting or drywall business, where you can be making a six-figure income or more, depending on where you live and how big you want to become.

You don't like any of my examples? Make up your own! Dream your own dreams — create your own reality. Don't punk out. I dare you to look inside yourself long enough to get a glimpse of your own secret dream. No dream is too big, too small, too dumb, or too outrageous.

Now, I want those of you who've had the guts to think about what you want to notice how you felt when you started to think about your future. Did you get discouraged or excited?

Were you able to visualize yourself doing the things you dream about? Or did you hear a little voice laughin' at you and sayin', "This is crazy." Are you embarrassed by your dreams? Do you think other people would think you weren't cool if they knew about your dreams for the future?

I'll bet some of you felt stupid and told yourselves that you could never succeed at gettin' what you want, 'cuz success is what happens to other people, not you.

Where's It Gonna Take You?

Don't think that becoming a successful businessman is bigger than it is. The main difference between workin' for a gang in the street and workin' in the straight world is where you end up when it's over.

If you're into any kind of illegal business, you have no future. You're livin' a temporary life-style, 'cuz you're gonna end up dead or in prison. On the other hand, if you invest in yourself and work as hard at creatin' a legal business as you have to in order to get over on the street, you can end up with a good life.

Straight companies and gangs aren't all that different from one another. Check out the chart.

Gang vs. Your Business		
Common Trait	**Gang**	**Your Business**
Name	Takes pride in name. Uses it to communicate something important about the gang and its members.	Takes pride in name. Nobody else can use it. Communicatesinformation about company and its products or services.
Specialized Market	Makes money by providing products or services to special markets (drugs, hot cars, etc.)	Makes money by providing products or services to special markets (computers, cars, etc.)
Territory	Stakes a claim to a specific area or territory, but has no ownership. Competes within the territory for the market share.	Competes with other companies within an area for market share. Territory not owned by company.
Image	Hairstyle, colors, gang signs, how you walk, how you talk, style and brand of clothes you wear, tattoos, type of car you drive, cell phone, beeper.	Hairstyle, language, body language, brand of clothes type of car you drive, computer, cell phone, beeper.

You Gotta Wanna,
'Cuz If You Don't Wanna, Ya Just Ain't Gonna

How do you get from where you are now to livin' your dream? Ya gotta wanna. Don't let other people tell you who you are and what you're able to accomplish. Decide that for yourself. You don't need a college degree, or a lot of money, or to be born in a certain neighborhood.

On the street it's called payin' your dues. In the straight world it's called education, and it comes in a lot of different forms. Things like readin' books, apprenticeships, on-the-job training, two- and four-year technical degrees, hangin' out with role models, and goin' to workshops and seminars. There's hundreds of business and self-help books, videos, and tapes that can help you get started *today*. Find out what you love to do in life, then find out what you'll need to succeed and go for it.

Think About It

- *It's now possible to make good money, runnin' your own business — makin' it outside the system, but inside the law.*
- *There are many kinds of education. Do yourself a favor, choose one.*
- *Dream your own dreams. Create your own reality. I dare you.*
- *Ya gotta wanna, 'cuz if you don't wanna, ya just ain' t gonna.*
- *Straight companies and gangs aren't all that different from one another.*

CHAPTER 17

Doin'
What Comes
Easy

Success Grows From
Things You're Already Good At

Remember when you were a little kid and people used to ask what you wanted to be when you grew up? Do you remember what you told them? Back then you didn't have to think too hard to come up with an answer. But if I were to ask you right now what you want to be or do with the rest of your life, I bet it'd be a lot harder for you to come up with an answer.

For some reason, it seems that the older we get, the more we lose touch with our dreams. We get so beaten down by our families and other people tellin' us that we can't do things, or how stupid our ideas are, that we end up losin' sight of all the possibilities we saw when we were little.

Natural Law

Many ancient cultures saw in nature a law of life some people call the Law of Least Resistance. This means that when we live according to our natural gifts, we're able to do less and accomplish more.

Look at nature. A tree doesn't try to be a tree. It's just a tree, and does what trees are supposed to do: provides food, shade, shelter, and oxygen for all living things. It doesn't take a lot of hard work and effort for a tree to be what it was created to be. Apple trees don't try to produce oranges, and pine trees don't try to produce apples. Each tree simply does what it was meant to do.

People are built the same way. We all have natural abilities. When we live and work according to our basic strengths and abilities, we're able to accomplish more with less effort. Knowing your natural strengths can change how you see yourself and your purpose.

That's great to say, but how do you figure out what your strengths are? Hang in there, and I'll show you a couple ways to help you find them.

First Let's Figure Out Your Style

Each of us have a certain style — how we dress and talk. We also have a special style for how we learn and experience life. Most people fit into one of three styles: visual (seeing), auditory (hearing) or kinesthetic (doing/feeling). No one style is better or worse than another.

Seeing

We're the guys who have to *see* for ourselves. If we had a motto, it'd be "Show me." For example, a person's facial expressions and body language tell me more than their words do. I always like to hold business meetings or important personal conversations face to face. That way I can *see* if a person is being open and honest with me, or if they're tryin' to b.s. me. When I watch a person, I'm able to know how far to push them, or when to back off; when to close a deal or when to blow it off.

For those of us who are *visual*, one of the first things we want to know when we buy a car is what it looks like. We have to be able to picture ourselves driving it.

We tend to move and think fast. We learn quickly and get bored easily. We understand and remember more of what we see than what we hear. If someone talks too slowly it drives us nuts. When I had a teacher in school who talked like that, I'd usually fall asleep.

Hearing
My friend Pete is like this. His motto is: "Let me hear you say it." If you're datin' a girl who is *auditory*, you'd better be watchin' what you say around her, and you'd better tell her regularly how much you care about her or she'll be history. She wants to *hear* how much you love her.

I've been married to two auditory women and believe me, auditory people listen intently to every word you say. Some of them are able to repeat to you word for word what you said six months or even three years later. Bein' visual, I have a tendency to forget what I've said the very next day. I learned the hard way I had to be very careful what I said, especially when we were fighting, 'cuz I'd likely hear about it later.

When my friend Pete buys a car, all he cares about is *hearin'* what it sounds like. He may or may not care what it looks like, but if the engine doesn't sound right, or if it doesn't have a great stereo system, he'll probably lose interest.

Teachers tend to be auditory. In fact, probably the majority of people make decisions based on what they *hear.*

Feeling
My friend Kruno didn't just want to read the directions or have somebody tell him how to do something. He learned and remembered best when he actually practiced it himself. His motto

was: "Let me do it myself."

When he bought a car, he liked to feel how comfortable it was. He'd run his hands along the lines of the car to get a feel for its design. He was interested in how the upholstery felt. He liked to get behind the wheel to feel how it handled.

Kinesthetic people usually feel things very deeply. Because of this, they can easily get their feelings hurt. They would usually rather lie than say something that would hurt someone, so they have a tendency to think before they speak. As a result, they usually talk slowly and deliberately.

If you're datin' a kinesthetic person, they like to be shown how much you care for them by being touched. They're often not impressed by how much you give them. They'll be quick to tell you that words are cheap. They want you to hold their hand, touch their arm, or cuddle a lot. This is what makes them feel valued and loved.

What Does It Mean?
It's easy to see why people fight so much when you understand that everybody has their own personal style. These different styles make us interpret each other's actions differently.

If an auditory teacher has five visual students and five kines-thetic students, the teacher and the students don't stand a chance with each other unless the teacher knows the different learning styles and can communicate using each one.

If I would've known about this while I was still in school, I think I might've had the guts to ask for help. But back then nobody knew about these different learning styles, so I grew up thinkin' I was stupid. It turns out that I just didn't learn the same way most of the other kids did.

Stand Up For Yourself

Don't let anybody rip off your education. If you're a visual learner and you're not gettin' it, talk to your teachers. Tell them you need to *see* what they're talkin' about — ask them to *show you what they mean.* If you're a kinesthetic learner, tell them you need to experience it before things make sense — ask them to *teach you how it works.* If you're auditory and you have a visual teacher who talks too fast and uses a lot of visual aids, go to that teacher and tell them you need them to *explain it to you.*

Look, everything in life is about our ability to relate and communicate. Being successful in school, at work, in relationships — or in life — comes from the ability to understand and communicate with each other. Knowin' about learning styles helps you understand yourself and other people better.

But what good is knowin' your style if you don't know what you're good at? Let's take a look at that next.

Think About It

- *Stand up for yourself. Don't let anybody rip off your education.*
- *It's easy to see why people fight so much when you understand that everybody has their own personal style. These styles make us interpret each other's actions differently.*
- *Success grows from things you're already good at.*

CHAPTER 18

So What Are You Good At?

Discover Your Strengths

We've looked at some of the ways we learn and relate to each other. Now we're gonna look at how we deal with life.

A friend of mine has discovered that there are four basic types of people (Creators, Advancers, Refiners, and Executors). He calls his system C.A.R.E. and teaches it to companies all over the world. And he makes big bucks doin' it.

Knowin' your own C.A.R.E. profile can help you see what your natural strengths and abilities are. It tells you the things you do better than other people, and helps you see where you fit in the best — what you're really good at. But most importantly, it helps you see that everybody's good at somethin' and that it takes everybody to get the job done.

Creator

Are you the one who comes up with the crazy ideas about what kind of job to pull or what to do on Saturday night? Do you get impatient or bored when you have to figure out all the details?

Do you come up with great ideas, but like to get other people to make 'em happen? Does an idea hit you, and then right away you're already thinkin' of three or four more? Do you like to break the rules? Then you're probably a *Creator.*

Ways To Make Money If You're a Creator

Product Development Specialist — How can you tell if this is you? Well, do you always think of ways you could make things better, funnier, faster, or more interesting when you're watchin' T.V. or walkin' down the street? Did you know that successful companies all over the world pay people a lot of money for developing new products and improving their old ones?

Think about it. TV, CD's, cars, and the Internet were all just someone's wild idea once. But some crazy mother ended up selling these new ideas and made a mint.

You can work in research and development for a company, or be a free agent and consult for many companies. You can come up with lots of different ideas for a company, or approach a company that you think could use an idea you have. Corporations might seem far from where you are right now, but if you're willing to dress and talk like them for a few hours a day, you'll see that it's an easy jump to make.

Advertising Agent — Ever had a commercial make you laugh? Ever thought a TV or radio ad was so stupid you could have come up with something better in your sleep? Ad agents make a lot of money, and their messages reach millions of people.

Consultant — Would you like to make money by going to a meeting with a client just to help them figure out how to solve their problems? Or how about hangin' out with people who are planning meetings and presentations? Would it be fun for you to help come up with ideas to make them more interesting and fun? Then you'd probably do well as a consultant.

Consultants usually work for themselves and sell their time to other people. They know how to solve problems or are able to come up with ideas that make other people's jobs easier or more profitable.

Consultants are used in every area of business: sales, manufacturing, marketing, management, public relations — and the list goes on and on. Top companies all over the country are dying to find people who are creative innovators. In fact, eighty-one percent of them think innovation is the thing that will promote their company's growth, but only six percent of them believe that their company is any good at it. Many executives are afraid that they're gonna go out of business if they can't find creative people who can help breathe new life into their companies.

Advancer

Or are you the guy who hears the great idea and instantly knows what needs to be done next? Can you see a lot of ways to get somethin' done? Do you know exactly who to call? Are you somebody who likes to change what the rules mean? If so, you're probably an *Advancer.*

Advancers are good at visualizing the master plan. When someone says that they have an idea, you tell them the people they should talk to or the things they should do next. If somebody has a bunch of new ideas, you usually know right away which ones will work. You'll even round up the right gang of guys to get it done. You're a gifted networker. You like to make things happen and are probably a natural at makin' money on the street.

I'm gonna let you in on a little secret: *Advancers* will succeed wherever they are. There are some great opportunities for you in the straight world, because you know how to plan, promote, and strategize.

Ways To Make Money If You're An Advancer

Sales — Just about every company has salespeople who usually work on commission. That means that you get part of everything you sell. Put on the right clothes and stop swearin', and you can make some serious cash.

Producer — Here's a glamorous, legal way to make some big bucks. Bring all the right people and things together to make somethin' happen, whether it's a movie, a CD, or anything else.

Agent / Promoter — It's no harder pushin' a client to studios or companies than it is pushin' dope. This way you can sleep at night and you're not facin' any hard time.

Mortgage Broker — These guys help people find the right mortgage for their house. I know an *Advancer* who pulls down $250,000 a year doing this. He takes three or four vacations a year to places like Jamaica and Cancun. This doesn't take a college education. You're just hookin' people up with the right bank and the right deal. But you do have to know how to read!

Stockbroker — The stock market can be a big gamble, but you can make a lot of money on it, too. Sellin' stocks is basically like most sales jobs, but I know of one guy who made $10 million in about 10 years because he had some friends who had really done their homework. And he didn't have to bury any of his money in the back yard — it was all perfectly legal.

Refiner

Do you tell everyone how the new idea's crazy and will never work? Can you see the hole in the plan that will make it fail? Do you like to be the one who makes everybody follow your rules? If this sounds like you, then you're probably a *Refiner.*

You can organize and correct things someone else messed up. You have the ability to keep track of a lot of details and can make sure things get done right. The *Creators* might think you're a downer, but they'd probably fail without you.

Ways To Make Money If You're A Refiner
A *Refiner* can work in a factory as a manager, in an office doing bookkeeping, or managing a system that gets done over and over. Or they could be an auto or bike mechanic, a plumber, a handyman, a housing contractor, a real estate appraiser, a teacher, or a private tutor. They could start their own cleaning or office organizing business. The list is endless.

Executor
Do you like to let others take the lead, but you know that they'd never really get anything done without you? Do you hate for things to always be changin'? Do you like to know exactly what you have to do before you try it? If you like to carry out someone else's big plan, as long as they tell you what to do, you're an *Executor*.

These people are good at mastering something that's done the same way every time, but they don't want to have to make choices or decisions for themselves. An *Executor* might like to pick locks, dismantle cars, crack safes, or even make a drop, as long as someone else takes care of the big picture for him.

Ways To Make Money If You're An Executor
In the straight world there are millions of jobs for *Executors*. Just decide if you like to do physical work, technical work (like building things or using computers), or work that involves people.

Do you like to mess around with computers? You could work as a computer technician, programmer, or do word processing and data entry.

Do you like the idea of providing support to someone who's a leader? Then you might enjoy being an administrative assistant.

How about workin' with numbers? Consider accounting or workin' for an organization like the IRS or H & R Block.
If you hate workin' inside, then there are lots of jobs you could do in the construction industry. Don't laugh. I know guys who make more than $100,000 a year runnin' construction crews, paintin' crews, and killin' bugs. And you know what? Just about every job I've mentioned could be turned into a business of your own.

Do you like people? You can make a lot of money by ownin' a business or service which does all the things that other people don't like or don't have time to do. *Executors* can be great service people and are good at jobs like phone and cable installation. Studies show that 80% of U.S. business is already in the service industry.

For instance, did you know that somebody in your city is makin' good money takin' care of potted plants, fish tanks, and large aquariums for doctors and other professional people who use them in their offices?

You Don't Like Any Of These Suggestions?
That's OK. The important thing is to do something you like. Sure, some people make a lot of money doin' what they don't like. But what a lousy way to spend your life. Success isn't just havin' a pile of money, it's enjoyin' what you do every day.

Is there something you think about all the time, like dancin', music, rappin', basketball, ways to sell things, or ways to convince others to do what you want? Any of these things can be turned into a way for you to make money.

Maybe you've never tried the thing you'll like the most. If you love to drive fast and take chances, you might want to join the

Air Force and become a fighter pilot. Don't ever think anything's too far out. The guy who started Federal Express, the first overnight delivery service, saw that a lot of people wanted to mail things at the last minute. He figured out a way for them to do it — and started a new billion-dollar industry. By the way, he developed his first business plan for FedEx as one of his college class assignments. His teacher gave him a "C" because she said it was too unrealistic and would never work. Think about what he would have missed if he had taken her word for it instead of followin' his dream.

Ever heard of CNN or Turner Broadcasting Company? Ted Turner, the man who started these companies, as well as other major television and movie production companies, is so rich that he gave a billion dollars to the United Nations last year.

A few years ago he even married Jane Fonda, a movie star he'd had a crush on his whole life. This guy's a real winner, right? Well, not long ago he said, "All my life people have said I wasn't going to make it." The reason he got everything he wanted was because he ignored all the jerks who tried to tell him his ideas were dumb and he couldn't succeed.

Be careful who you listen to. Don't let anyone stop your dreams.

Think About It

- *When we live according to our basic strengths and abilities, we can accomplish more with less effort.*
- *Everybody's good at something. What is it for you?*
- *You have a lot of legal options for makin' good money — and enjoyin' what you do.*

CHAPTER 19

Where You Gonna Go From Here?
From Drug Dealer
To
Being Your Own Boss

**"I can tell you how to get rich in nine months.
But the nine-month plan ends in a funeral."**
Ice-T
December 9,1996

You've Already Got What It Takes
To Build a Successful Business
*If you've been successfully flippin' dope, then you've
organized, managed, and assumed the risks of your own
business. You've created a business and made it work.*

So what does that mean? I'm gonna say it one more time: it
means you've got what it takes to build a successful legal business. Because the skills needed to be successful in a legal business or an illegal business are *exactly the same.*

From A Taste Of The Good Life
To All You Can Eat
I have to admit that when I first started writin' this book I assumed most of you out there would pick it up out of curiosity;

that in the beginning you'd just want to see what this crazy sucker had to say!

But I didn't stop there. Since then, I've made some other assumptions: that if you're still hangin' with me, it's because you really do wanna get control of your life, that you want a good life for yourself, and that you'd like to get off the street and live past 30.

It's Your Right To Dream
Of Havin' What You Want
Wait! Before you go off on me — think about it. That's pretty much everybody's dream.

Just try to find even *one* bad mother out there workin' the street that doesn't dream about that one big score that'll make it possible to someday leave it all behind. Most people want to make as much money as fast as they can, and then get out.

Even some of the big Mafia families, as soon as they could, put money and energy into legal businesses because they wanted a better life for their children. They didn't want their sons to be involved with the illegal family businesses. They wanted them to be respectable, legitimate businessmen, 'cuz anyone who's been on the streets for very long knows that the gangster life is not the good life. And isn't that why we all tell ourselves we're out there, to get a taste of the good life for ourselves and our families?

Biggie Smalls' Dream Was To Get Outta The Street
Before his death, Gangsta Rapper Biggie Smalls told an interviewer, "I used to do a whole lot of f— up s—...I'm just tryin' to blossom more into being a father and a man...more than just...out there wildin'...I don't want m———f—— to just look at Big and be like, 'Oh s—, there go Big, the dope emcee.' I want people to look at Big like, *'Look at Big. He grew. He's a businessman now. He's a father now. He's takin' control of his*

destiny. He's movin' up. He's not the same...dude no more.' Every night before I go to sleep (I think about what's next). I definitely want to relocate. Somewhere in the South. Somewhere where life is a little bit slower. Where I can just move at my pace...I just wanna be in a calm area. I just wanna be able to relax... I wasn't thinking, 'One day I'm gonna get rich and still live in the hood.' My dream house has a picket fence and green grass. I picture my daughter playin' out in my backyard on the swing and on the jungle gyms."

Even Notorious B.I.G.'s dream was to get out of the street and move on to more peaceful surroundings. On March 9, 1997, Christopher Wallace, a.k.a. Notorious B.I.G., left the street and gangster life for good. He was killed in a drive-by shooting in LA. He got out, but not exactly the way he had planned.

It Don't Happen Overnight
Eventually, almost everybody retires from the streets — either voluntarily or involuntarily by gettin' busted or killed.

You're at the place in your life where you still have a choice. You can still do what Biggie was in the process of doin'. You can take back control of your own destiny!

Notice I said that Biggie was in the *process* of takin' back control of his own destiny. It doesn't happen overnight; not for anybody.

If you don't believe anything else I've said to you, believe this: you can dream big dreams and make all of the right choices, but unless you understand that life is a process — a journey, not a destination — you won't have the patience and persistence you're gonna need in order to grow into your dreams. But you've already got what it takes to begin: the ability to dream, the power to choose, and time.

Wastin' Time

Every day that you're not goin' after what you want is a wasted day. Most of us waste time believin' we don't have what it takes to have the kind of life we dream of. We're told that we're no-good, worthless bums so often that we give up on our dreams and turn to crime instead — thinkin' it'll give us at least a taste of the good life.

If you're like I used to be, down deep you probably believe that you're a no-good, worthless scumbag. You don't dare believe that you'll ever be able to do anything worthwhile, because you've bought into the negative b.s. other people say to you, and about you, instead of lookin' at the facts.

You Gotta Believe It's OK For You To Succeed

Now, in the last chapter, you learned that everyone has a specialty —something that they're really good at. By now I hope you're startin' to recognize what that is for you.

There's just one thing: *ya gotta wanna get off the streets bad, because it takes a lot of courage and practice to change how you see yourself.*

It's not enough to be told what you *can* do. In your heart you gotta really believe that *it's OK* for you to succeed at what you're good at — otherwise you won't be able to picture yourself havin' the life you want.

And if you can't see yourself bein' happy and successful, chances are you never will be. If you think you're no good, you'll probably end up with nothin'.

You know what? If I'd spent as much time and energy believin' that I could succeed as I did believin' I was a failure, I'd have saved myself a whole lot of time, pain, and trouble. It took me almost ten years to finally get it. You're luckier than I was. You've got a head start. You can figure it out faster than I ever did.

How To Begin — Dare To Dream
The first thing you have to do is decide whether you're a nickel and dime sucker who's willin' to sell out by doin' everything halfway; or whether you're gonna take yourself to a successful place where you belong.

I mean, who are you, and what is your purpose for being here? What's your dream?

Look around you, man. What you see and hear from society — that you're a no-good, worthless punk who'll never amount to anything — is a lie. That's not who you are and why you're here. You gotta look somewhere else for that answer. *You gotta look inside yourself.*

Go on, I dare you to look past the anger. Look past the fear. *What's your dream?* What do *you* want to do with your life? Where would *you* like to be in five years; what about ten years?

If all you want is to be sittin' in the joint doin' five to ten, that's OK. I just want to make sure that you're awake, and know what it is you're choosin'.

Stop Hangin' Out With Fools
Now, the next thing you need to do is find somebody successful you can talk to who's goin' in the same direction you've chosen to go. And as much as possible, ignore all those fools who tell you that you can't make it — even if those people are your parents, or your teachers, or your friends.

When I decided to stop dealin' drugs, the first thing I did was find new people to hang out with. I began spendin' time with some professional men from a support group I went to.

Now believe me, these guys were geeks! They were the kind of guys I had always made it a habit to avoid — super-straight professional types. In the beginning I was really worried about how they would handle it when they found out who I was, and what I did for a livin'.

Remember, I said that takin' control of your own life is a process, and believe me, I was in the very early stages of that process when I met these guys. I hadn't totally quit the dope business. I was just investigatin' some new possibilities when I met them.

But you know what? I got the surprise of my life! They didn't laugh. They didn't go into shock. They didn't call the cops. They didn't ask me to leave. Instead, they opened their hearts to me, and drew me into their circle. They recognized the courage it took for me to even show up at their meetings, and they gave me 100% of their support. In fact, those geeks became my new best friends. They encouraged me and cheered me on. They dared me to see myself through new eyes.

New Connections —
Find a Mentor Or a Teacher
When I was in my late teens and early twenties, I spent a very short time in commission sales. At the time, I was still hung up on my old speech problem and didn't like myself very much. I was paranoid to talk to new people, because I was afraid that I'd choke and blow it. But since I had experienced such success in drug sales, I was confident enough to take a chance on legit sales again.

Failin' The Test By Tryin' To Be a Good Guy
The first sales job I applied for turned out to be a disaster. The company sold food products to grocery stores, and it was their policy to give prospective employees a test that was supposed to let them know if they would do well in commission sales.

At my final interview I was told that, accordin' to the test I had taken, I wasn't a risk taker, and wouldn't be good at sales. Well, the laugh was on me, because I had worked so hard at answerin' the questions the way I thought *they* would think was correct that I didn't tell them the truth. What a joke! Imagine me bein' told by some geek sittin' behind a desk that *I'm* not a risk taker. Here I was with a 9-millimeter under my arm, and two kilos of coke, and $100,000 in the trunk of my car, but their test told them that I wasn't enough of a risk taker to work for their company. Go figure!

If You Can't See Yourself, Find Someone Who Can

Fortunately, not long after this I met a guy by the name of Danny Falk, the owner of DLF Machine Tools. Danny saw in me things I couldn't see in myself. Here he was, a very successful business owner, but he believed in me more than I could believe in myself.

He used to tell me, "Ron, you have more enthusiasm than anyone I've ever met! And you have incredible drive...you're like a diamond in the rough. All I have to do is polish you, buddy." So he enrolled me in the "Danny Falk School of Salesmanship," and for two years he worked on me.

I didn't know what I was gettin' myself into. I just knew that here was a highly successful man who was willin' to teach me everything he knew about bein' a successful salesperson, and I wasn't stupid enough to pass up this chance.

When I had first gotten into the drug business, I looked for old timers who knew the business inside and out, and I learned everything I could from them. From my street experience I had learned that if you want to be the best, you have to learn from the best.

I stayed with Danny a couple of years before I decided that I was ready to go out on my own, and I'll never forget what I learned while workin' with him. He gave me confidence I'd never have gotten on my own.

Some Guys I've Known Who've Made It
The following names have been changed to protect the guilty as well as the innocent.

Look, I'm not special. There are a lot of other guys out there who've gotten off the streets, who've become successful, and who are livin' a good life.

From Minimum Wage To $150,000 a Year
Take my friend Kenny, for instance. Here's a guy who, back in the early eighties, had one of the biggest drug distribution networks in the Midwest.

But he woke up! He spent one day too many in the joint and figured that there had to be a better way to live. So he looked around, and decided that instead of contracting big dope deals, he was gonna learn how to be a building contractor.

He didn't start out makin' big money bein' a contractor. He took the first few years just learnin' the construction business from the ground up. In the beginning he worked as a day laborer for minimum wage. But he went from laborer to crew chief, to subcontractor, to contractor. Just like he had done in the dope business, he paid his dues. Today he has twenty guys workin' for him, and he makes about $150,000 a year doin' commercial remodeling jobs.

Billy The Bug Man
Or what about my friend Billy the Bookie? After about five years in the business he realized that there was only one future workin' outside the law, and the retirement plan wasn't all that

appealin'.

A friend of his told him that there was good money to be made in commercial and residential pest extermination. Now this wasn't exactly his idea of a good time, but he figured out that if he was willin' to start out at the bottom and learn the business, in five years he could have his own extermination company and hire other people to do the actual extermination work.

That's exactly what he did. Instead of Billy the Bookie, he's now known as Billy the Bug Man.

Laugh if you want to. But nobody who knows him is laughin', because he now owns one of the largest extermination companies in Wisconsin, and he makes more money than he ever did makin' book.

Crazy Charley Was Smarter Than I Thought

Crazy Charley was another guy I knew when I was in the dope business. He used to do quite a good little business for me, so I was really surprised and kinda mad the day he told me that he was gettin' out of the business. At first I thought he'd been busted, but he told me no, that he'd decided to go to work for his brother-in-law paintin' houses.

I told him I thought he was nuts! Why would anybody doin' as good as he was want to get out of the business? But he had made up his mind, and there was nothin' I could do to change it.

All I could think was what a chump he was to be willin' to work for almost nothin' as a painter. But I was dead wrong. Today he has seven people workin' for him, and he makes $75,000 a year doin' residential and commercial jobs, and he ain't lookin' over his shoulder anymore.

Every One Of These Guys Started Off Small

They figured out what they wanted to do and were willin' to start at the bottom, learn the business, and work their way up as an apprentice. Each of them wanted to be his own boss. They all learned the basics and then they learned the shortcuts. They learned how their bosses marketed themselves, what kind of advertising worked best (word of mouth, newspaper ads, magazine ads, etc.). When they figured they were ready, they each took the risk to go into business on their own. *Each got to experience the adrenaline rush you get when you start your own business.*

There's No Such Thing As a Free Ride
It's easy to get into the dope business. The hard part is how you get out.

I get real tired hearin' about how easy it is to be successful, either in the dope business or in a straight business. That's b.s.! Every time I go to schools or detention centers to talk, the first thing out of some kid's mouth is, "Where we gonna make this kinda money so quick?"

They don't ever talk about the heavy losses you take when your people get busted with your product. They don't ever wanna talk about gettin' ripped off, or people not payin', or gettin' killed. The dope business is a business with high risks and big losses. And unlike in the straight world, ya can't cry to the cops. When trouble comes, you gotta pay to have it taken care of yourself.

Nobody wants to talk about how it takes four or five years to really start makin' money flippin' dope. You're not gonna start out connectin' with big money deals right away, unless it's a set-up. And if it is, you're in deep trouble.

It's not any easier to be a successful drug dealer than it is to be successful in any other business. In fact, it's probably harder! There's a heck of a lot more workin' against your success on the streets than there is in the straight world.

There's just no such thing as a free ride — not in the world of legitimate business, and not on the street. A lot of time, energy, and hard work go into any success.

As Ice-T said, "...why get into a profession where you can't win?"

Think About It

- *Takin' back control of your own destiny happens one step at a time. It doesn't happen overnight.*
- *Don't be a sucker. The ultimate scam is to buy into the negative stuff other people say to you or about you.*
- *There's no such thing as a free ride. Not on the street, and not in the straight world.*
- *There's a lot more workin' against your success on the street than in the straight world — so why get into a profession where you can't win?*
- *Look past your anger and fear to find your dream — I dare you!*

CHAPTER 20

Give Yourself
A
Break

Everybody needs a break, so start out by givin' yourself one. 'Cuz if you don't, who will?

There's a lot of competition out there, and you need to give yourself every advantage you can. So start by believin' in yourself!

Now, don't go gettin' all freaked out about the competition. You gave yourself a head start when you started readin' this book! By now you've decided you want to get ahead or you wouldn't still be readin'.

Most people are quitters. They either didn't bother pickin' up the book or didn't make it past the first chapter. Congratulate yourself and keep readin'. You're already ahead of the pack.

You're not alone in this process. Down the road you're gonna be surprised by how many people will be on your side, cheerin' you on. You've got what it takes to do anything you set your heart on. So don't hold back — go for it all.

It's not enough just for me to believe in you. You gotta believe in yourself enough to start takin' control of your own life.

One way you can do this is by settin' goals for yourself.

Knowing Where You Wanna End Up

Goals are like targets. If you're out on the shootin' range and you're aimin' at nothin', that's what you're gonna hit — *nothin'.* Without them, you're just wanderin' around, goin' nowhere, aimin' at nothin'. And that's exactly what you get: *nowhere, with nothin'.*

If you don't know where you're goin', how ya gonna know when you get there? Decidin' where you wanna end up lets you know if you're aimin' in the right direction. *It gives you more control over what happens to you. So stop bein' a victim and thinkin' that things just happen to you.*

Man, there's more to your life than just today. What do you want to be? Where do you want to live? What kind of life do you want to have for yourself?

Start out by settin' small goals that'll be easy for you to reach. Look at where you are right now compared to where you wanna be. Plan how you're gonna get there from here. If you don't know the right steps to take, then ask somebody who's already gotten there — or who is a couple of steps closer to gettin' there than you. What have you got to lose?

Don't freak out and quit if you don't get where you wanna be the first time around. Just learn what you can, adjust and keep goin'. Gettin' there happens one step at a time, one day at a time. You're not gonna get there overnight. Nobody does. But if you're doin' what you like, you'll enjoy every step and every day.

Hangin' With The Big Boys
Is About Attitude And Image

The Right Look

If you're in a gang you know about look; it's the way you wear your hair, your gang signs, your colors, how you talk, how you walk, your tattoos, the brand of clothes you wear and how you wear them.

Is this a big deal? You better believe it. Image or look isn't somethin' we're born with. It's somethin' we create to show other people who we are and what we're about.

What would happen if some geek showed up in your neighborhood wearin' a suit and tie? You'd think he's an undercover cop, a probation officer, a DEA agent or a social worker. Would you trust him and want to hang out with him? No way! You'd either kick his butt or stay far away from him because the guy doesn't look and act like somebody you can trust.

But what if this same guy showed up lookin' and talkin' like a brother? You might not take him in right away, but at least you'd be willin' to give him a chance because the image he was projectin' was familiar to you.

The same's true for the straight world. If you try to get certain jobs and show up wearin' baggy jeans and colors, at best they'll think you're an idiot, and at worst they'll think you're a gangster. Either way, you're out on your butt because your image is workin' against you. You may be the best person for the job, but if you're not able to package yourself in a way that tells people you've got somethin' to offer, you'll probably miss out on a chance to show what you can really do.

Today lots of companies spend hundreds of thousands of dollars creatin' an image they believe will attract customers. They communicate this image in their offices, their advertising, the products or services they sell, and *how their employees look and act*. Can you blame a company for not wantin' to hire someone they think sounds stupid or looks dangerous?

If You've Got The Right Look, You Can Get Away With a Lot

I know a guy who was an advertising genius. He used to go into companies with long hair, a beard, and wild clothes, and the stuffy business owners never bought his ideas.

Then one day he saw a guy on a talk show who'd written a book about dressin' for success. This guy said that people listen to you more when you dress like *their idea* of success. He figured he didn't have anything to lose, so he cut his hair, got rid of the beard, bought some really cool ties and the sharpest suit he could find.

All of a sudden, the stuffy old business guys stopped callin' his ideas risky and started sayin' he was "cutting edge." He was still the same guy, but now they trusted him because *he looked the way they thought a successful advertising man should look.* They stopped focusing on how he looked and started concentrating on what he could do for them. My friend began to make some serious money and ended up winning lots of advertising awards. And all he changed was how he looked when he was working.

Your look can either work for you or against you. It's all about bein' able to blend with your environment. When you're hangin' with your friends you dress and act one way, but when you're workin' with the public and it's about business, you gotta have a professional image. You gotta leave your hangin' out clothes and street language at home.

Lookin' Like You Belong Is Only Half The Battle

There's a story about a wealthy English guy who wanted to

prove that his friends cared more about appearances than they did about who a person really was.

So he found a dirty young street girl and bet his brother that he could pass her off as a princess. He taught her high-class manners, dressed her in expensive gowns, and taught her how to talk and walk like an upper-class woman. Finally it was time to prove his point. He took her to a big party and introduced her as his cousin. She was so perfect they thought she really was a princess. It was all about image and style — not just how she looked, but how she talked, moved, and acted.

You don't have to change into some weird geek. You just have to wear the right clothes and act the right way for the business you're in.

Your business style will be determined by what your customers expect. For example, if you're tryin' to sell feed to a dairy farmer, you wouldn't get very far if you show up at his place dressed in a $2000 suit, wearin' $250 Italian leather shoes, drivin' a foreign car, and talkin' like a New York lawyer. And when you go to the doctor, you don't expect him to show up lookin' like he just walked out of prison.

It's like this. When you're workin' with people, it's important for them to have confidence in your ability to do a good job or sell them good products.

Whether we like it or not, first impressions are very important in the business world. Usually you only have one chance to sell yourself or your products to a customer. If you blow it the first time, it's hard to get a second chance.

You may have noticed that the first time you meet someone, you decide what they're about in the first two minutes. Those first couple of minutes leave a lasting impression.

How You Talk Makes a Difference

How I talk has been a real problem for me, so don't think I'm judgin' you or puttin' you down when I tell you these things.

Whether you like it or not, the words you use in any business are very important. They can make people trust and believe in you, or mistrust you, or dislike you. *Remember, people part with their money when they feel comfortable. So you want people to feel good enough about you to be willin' to give you their business.*

This has been a hard one for me. I grew up on the street, so for more than twenty-five years everything that came out of my mouth was street language. When I left the life, I had to learn a whole new way of talkin'.

I learned new words and their meanings, so I could improve my ability to talk to people in the business world. It was like I was livin' in a foreign country. If I had moved to Italy or Germany I couldn't expect them to understand English. I'd have to learn their language before I could communicate with them.

Think about it. How would you react to some guy on the street who talks like a Harvard college geek? Would you think he had any street smarts? You'd probably feel like he's talkin' down to you, and that he thought he was better than you.

Street language is a powerful way of communicatin', but it's like a foreign language to most people in the straight world. That's why so many social workers and probation officers fail. They come into their new jobs right out of college with big hearts, but all they know is what they've read in books. They don't speak our language and don't know what it's like to be on the street. And we hate it when people don't bother learnin' who we are. When they don't learn how to communicate with us, it sets up a barrier. We feel like they're lookin' down on us, so we retaliate by connin' them and tryin' to get over on them. Then they get ticked off at us and don't trust us. Eventually they get burned out with their jobs.

DEA agents and some cops have figured this out, and that's why some of them succeed. They've learned the language and rhythm of the streets so they blend into the neighborhood, and people are more willin' to deal with them. Don't misunderstand what I'm sayin' here. I'm not raggin' on the cops or social workers. Like in any other business, there's some good ones and there's some bad ones.

The same is true with us. There's a lot of us who try to go into the straight world without tryin' to learn the language. We think we're cool and they'd better accept us the way we are. This causes a lot of friction between us. But instead of just dealin' with it by learnin' the professional language, we give up and drop out.

They don't learn our language and we don't learn theirs. They think we're too crude and vulgar, and we think that they're jerks. And so we go on, year after year, makin' each other wrong.

Learn To Be a Master Of Disguise

Don't be afraid to learn their language and dress their style, and don't be afraid of blendin' eight to ten hours a day in the straight world. When you go home at night you can put on your other clothes, unwind with the brothers, and be yourself. Lots of people I know do this.

I'm not sayin' one way of talkin' is better than another. But I *am* tellin' you to be adaptable. Learn how to communicate in all types of situations with all types of people.

If you have a problem with writing or speaking, or don't have a high school diploma, or you've got a drug or alcohol dependency or a prison record, then you've got some obstacles to overcome. But so what? These things can't keep you from havin' a successful, long life unless you let 'em. Yeah, you're gonna need some extra help in the beginnin'. But there's nothin' uncool about needin' help unless you're too chicken to ask for it.

If you fell out of a boat in the middle of a lake and couldn't swim, would you go ahead and drown because you were too cool to ask for help? Or would you be screamin' that you're drownin' to anybody who'd listen? You wouldn't quit just because the first person you ask for help either didn't hear you or couldn't help you. You'd keep yellin' until you got some help.

Well, a whole lot of you chumps out there are goin' down for the third time. If you don't start reachin' out, askin' for the help you need, it's gonna be too late — you're gonna drown out there on the sea of life because you were too cool to get some help. What's that about?

Attitude Can Make You Or Break You
Man, in business your attitude can make you or break you. Think about all those jerks who've copped a 'tude or dissed you. You probably wanted to do 'em right there. You sure didn't wanna give 'em any of your money.

Nobody wants to work with some lazy punk who think's he's always right. Learn to play the people game. If somebody thinks differently than you, take the time to listen. Their ideas might make your idea better. Everybody wants to be heard. You do, too. So help them hear you by first hearin' them. That way you'll help people feel good about givin' you their business, because you're treatin' them with respect and dignity. That goes for your employer or your customer. Remember: you can draw a lot more flies with honey than you can with vinegar.

Think About It

- If you don't give yourself a break, who will?
- The only person who can stop you from bein' successful is you.
- Image isn't somethin' we're born with, it's somethin' we create .
- If you don't know where you're goin', how ya gonna know when you get there?
- There's more to life than just today. What do you wanna be ?
- Street language is a powerful way of communicating, but it doesn't fit in the business world 'cuz so many people don't understand it.
- Don't be afraid of learnin' how to talk like people in the straight world. It'll give you flexibility and make them want to trust you.
- Do everything you can to help people feel good about doin' business with you.

PART FIVE:

Makin' It Work

CHAPTER 21

My Last Days
As A Punk

Hittin' Bottom — The Last 12 Months

When you finally hit bottom, you start thinkin' maybe somethin' *is* wrong.

Nobody stays on top forever, and when I started my downward spiral it was a slow, painful fall to the bottom. So many of my real friends and best connections were either dead, in the joint or on the run that it was gettin' harder and harder to know who I could really count on. My life sure wasn't what I expected it to be when I first started out in the dope business.

I was on probation for a b.s. charge; my relationship with my wife was at an all-time low; and my coke habit was way out of control and was affecting my personal life and my business decisions. I was makin' a lot of stupid mistakes — breakin' too many of my own business rules. And you know what? I didn't care. I just didn't care. I was sick of everything and everybody. This is usually a good sign that something's gotta change.

An Early Morning Raid On My House

By this time, the cops were real anxious to bust me. They'd

been watchin' me for a long time, but so far had not been able to get much on me.

My brother-in-law had been flippin' pot for me for several years, when one day he came to me because he had a buyer for a couple of ounces of coke. I told him there was no way I'd give him that much coke — he'd have to start out slow. Johnny swore he knew the buyer and that he was alright. But I told him I didn't care, I'd only give him a quarter ounce 'cuz he didn't know enough about the coke business and there was too much at stake. The rules were different and the risks were greater in the coke business. I'd start him off small so he could learn what he was doin'.

Johnny arrived at the KMart parkin' lot to deliver the quarter ounce of coke to his buddy. Sure enough, the guy turned out to be an undercover narcotics agent, and the cops hauled Johnny's butt to jail. They did everything they could to get him to turn over on me, but he wouldn't.

The agents who'd been stakin' him out saw him drop by my house just before he made his delivery. They convinced some judge that this was enough to get a search warrant.

Well, these suckers showed up at my house at three o'clock that mornin'. For some reason, before they busted in, I woke up and looked out my window. Outside it was like the television police drama, *Cops*. Law enforcement officers were everywhere I looked — city cops, DEA — you name it, they were there.

I woke up my wife and told her that we were bein' raided. Of course she freaked out. I opened the front door and a half a dozen officers pointed guns at my head. I was informed that I was under arrest for sellin' a quarter ounce of cocaine to my brother-in-law. They shoved me to the floor and cuffed me, and then brought Linda out and had her sit on the couch. I didn't know it at the time, but my oldest son, Jay, woke up and came out and saw me lyin' face down on the floor. The cops let Linda put him back to bed.

For the next four hours the cops tried to get Linda and me to tell them where I hid my coke. I collected guns, and at the time I had about 35 or 40. It didn't take them long to find my guns, some cut, my scales, and a little pot. The also found $550 in my pants pocket from the sale of the quarter ounce of cocaine.

One of the cops came in and told me he'd found my guns, but couldn't find the coke, and insisted that I tell him where it was stashed. I said, "Forget it," so he started slappin' me. Here I was, sittin' next to my wife on the couch with my hands cuffed behind my back and my legs shackled, and he was workin' me over.

It got to be ridiculous. About every fifteen minutes somebody would come in and demand that we tell 'em where the coke was. I'd call them every punk name I could think of, and they'd knock me around, then go back to lookin' for the dope. Finally, after two hours of diggin' through my house, they finally found two ounces I had stashed in a coffee can on top of my refrigerator.

The way they acted, you'd have thought they had just run across a warehouse belongin' to one of the Colombian Cartel. Boy, was I relieved! I was hopin' they'd find that stash instead of the two pounds I had hangin' in my snowmobile suit downstairs in a closet. I kept tellin' 'em that was all I had. After another two hours they quit lookin'.

Somebody Must've Been Watchin' Out For Me
They had my scales, 35 guns, a pound of cut, two ounces of coke, the marijuana, and my account books with names, addresses, phone numbers, monies owed, and delivery dates. But in all the excitement, somebody laid the books down on top of a dresser and forgot about 'em. Talk about a break. If they

had taken my books, they really would have had me.

You gotta remember we were in a suburb of Milwaukee, and this was one of the biggest drug busts they'd ever made up to that point. The cops had all those guns and two ounces of coke. They were so happy they got me, they were actin' like it was Christmas.

My quiet, upper middle class neighbors were in for a shock. They had no idea what was goin' on until they read about it on the front page of the New Berlin and Menomonee Falls newspapers.

The cops had been after me for a long time, and now they thought they had me. They questioned me for hours, but all I'd say was I wanted to talk to my attorney. I had a real cocky attitude. I told them they had nothin' on me, and that I'd be out of there in a day.

My lawyer showed up and told me that for a $15,000 retainer he'd have me walkin' the streets by Monday. This was on Friday.

I spent the weekend in jail because my probation officer refused to come and see me so I could be released. I used to torment the guy, so that was his payback.

Do you remember the word "technicality"? Well, Monday morning my attorney got all charges dropped because the warrant had been obtained without probable cause. It was issued simply because my brother-in-law had walked into my house. That wasn't enough reason to suspect me of a crime. He came to my house all the time — after all, he was my brother-in-law.

I don't want to leave you thinkin' that this was no big deal. It was a very big deal. It shook me and everybody else up. This bust cost me a lot, and I'm not referrin' just to the money. In fact, one of my closest buddies, Skid the Kid, quit the business when I got busted. The clock was tickin' and my time was runnin' out.

My Nightmare Begins

I can't say it enough: my life was out of control. I was a nightmare to be around and had unpredictable mood swings. My wife was sick of our life, and my kids were scared to death of me. They stayed as far away from me as possible. I acted like I didn't care about them or anybody else. I was explosively abusive.

I had become my dad, and I didn't even know it.

I was in a fog, I couldn't think straight. Nothin' mattered very much anymore.

I'll never forget the day my wife asked me to leave and never come back. On one level I felt relieved, but it also hurt me bad. I wanted to love her and my boys, but I just didn't know how.

When we separated, the lawyers set up regular times when I would be allowed to spend time with my kids. I really missed them, and looked forward to the first weekend we'd spend together. Then it hit me. I didn't even know how to be with them. I began to realize that I had never spent time with them before. I started to panic. What was I gonna do with an 11, 7, and 3-year-old?

I did the only thing I could think of. I went downstairs to my friend's apartment and asked his wife what I should do with my kids. At first I think she thought I was kiddin', but it didn't take her long to see that I really didn't know what to do with three boys.

I'll always be grateful for what she told me that day: the only secret to bein' with kids is just to *be* with them — take them to the park, play basketball, feed the ducks — hang out. And that's what we did.

The trouble is, I wasn't used to hangin' out with them, and they were still scared to death of me. They had to learn to trust me one day at a time. I had to get used to bein' a real father for the first time in my life. It was hard for all of us. It took at least two years for us to learn how to be comfortable together.

There Are a Lot Of Different Ways To Die

My home life wasn't the only thing that was fallin' apart. That year I learned that there's a lot of different ways to die — and that whether it's deliberate or accidental, suicide or a professional hit, you wind up just as dead.

You can be talkin' on the phone and OD with a needle in your arm, like my friend Wild Man did, or you can attach one end of a string to the trigger of a shotgun and the other end to your big toe and blow your own brains out, like Wild Man's old lady did.

In fact, your brains will drip off the ceilin' whether you use a shotgun or a 45 — it's just a whole lot messier when you use a shotgun. I found that out a couple months later, when one of my guys blew his brains out just before I arrived to take him and his partner to catch a plane to New York City. They were gonna make a score for us. We never did figure out what it had been about. We didn't have a clue he was plannin' to check out on us.

Then there was Shorty. He and a friend of his had set up what was supposed to be a half-million dollar coke deal down in Florida. But the deal turned sour, and Shorty ended up gettin' killed. A few weeks later we learned that it had been his good friend who had set him up for the money. There never had been any coke deal.

If guns aren't your thing, you can do what my friend Kruno did. He got so drunk he couldn't see straight and drove off an overpass bridge. Kruno didn't really mean to kill himself, but he ended up just as dead. He was so wasted that he lost control of his car and swerved into an oncoming truck. The impact flipped his vehicle over the bridge and he was killed instantly.

If none of these ideas suits you, you could always rat on some guys to the DEA, then tell them to go screw themselves, and wait around town until they blow your face off in front of your own house — like they did to JR.

I was surrounded by death. I can't even remember the names of all the brothers I lost that year.

Friends —
Sometimes They're Enemies In Disguise

Death wasn't the only way I lost friends that year. Word got around fast that I was losin' my edge and my inner circle. I didn't know it at the time, but I wasn't thinkin' straight and had become vulnerable to attack from the outside. A couple of guys I thought were my friends just couldn't pass up the opportunity to set me up and rip me off. I lost almost $100,000 to these punks. With friends like these, I didn't need enemies. If I'd been straight, they'd never have been able to pull it off. But like I said before, that White Lady had my nose wide open and she was doin' all my thinkin'.

I Didn't Even Care That I Didn't Care

The sad truth is, I'd forgotten how to care. I was out of control. I didn't like or trust anybody anymore. I couldn't even trust my own brother Richie. He'd gotten so strung out on heroin that all he could do was think about feedin' that monkey he had ridin' his back. We were some kind of a team — him and his monkey, and me and my White Lady.

I hated my life. The harder I worked to get things under control, the worse things got. It was like tryin' to hold a cup of sand in my hand and keep it from seepin' out between my fingers.

That White Lady Had My Nose Wide Open

By this time, I had totally lost any edge I'd ever had. Most of my profits were goin' in my vein, or up my nose.

Business had changed; my coke habit had changed; I had changed. I wasn't the smart new guy on the block anymore. Instead, I was strung out on coke and had become an arrogant, paranoid shell of my former self. I had all the money I wanted in the world, but I couldn't spend it. Spiritually I was bankrupt. Emotionally I was hurtin' and didn't care if I died.

Even my body was out of control. Here I was surrounded by beautiful women who'd do anything for some coke, and I couldn't do anything about it. I'd lost my dignity, my family, my manhood, and my mind. I had everything I thought I had ever wanted, and yet I was worse off than I'd ever been in my life. I didn't know who I was anymore.

Everything was crashin' down around me. I didn't know what was real anymore. I was haunted by nightmares. Every time the phone rang I broke into a sweat — afraid to hear that someone else had been busted or blown away, or had decided to snitch on me.

No matter how hard I worked, or how many deals I tried to put together, nothin' seemed to go right. Everything was gettin' tougher — the cops, the courts, and the criminals. The rules had changed on the street and in the courtroom. The enormous profit potential of the cocaine business had created deadly competition in the street. Things had gotten to the point where too often the rule was kill or be killed.

At a time when I needed to be at the top of my game, I was worn out and paranoid. I was so sick of life that one day I sat down at my kitchen table, put my nine-millimeter in my mouth, and was about to pull the trigger. That's when I heard something inside me say, "There's got to be somethin' more to life than this. There's just got to be."

I got up and walked out the door, afraid that if I stayed at that table another minute, I wouldn't live long enough to find out what it was.

Facin' The Facts: My First Look At What I'd Become
That night it happened — the thing that changed my life forever.

I decided to stop off at one of my favorite hangouts, hopin' to catch up with Skid the Kid. I was messed up and depressed, so it was good to see him walk in. Skid had been one of my most trusted friends and business associates — though lately I hadn't seen much of him.

We sat for a while just drinkin' and talkin'. One thing led to another and before I knew it, I was tellin' him how bad things were and how miserable I was. I had always been able to confide in Skid. He was a good listener and a sympathetic friend, and I didn't expect today to be any different.

But the more I talked, the quieter he got. Finally, he looked me straight in the eye and said, "Look, man, I don't want to hear it anymore. What's the matter with you? You're nothin' anymore. You've become one of the scumball derelict junkies you used to make fun of. You're the lowest of the low.

"You've gotten so out of control that I never know anymore if you're gonna lose your temper and blow me away or somehow get us both blown away. You're dangerous, man. I can't trust you anymore. You're no fun to be around.

"You may not care whether you live or die, but I have a family! It's clear to me that you don't care about yourself or anybody else anymore. You need help, brother, and if you can't or won't get help, then you need to stay away from me and my family, cuz we're not goin' down with you."

He stood up, took a card out of his pocket, and threw it on the table. "You're paranoid. You've lost your edge. Here's a guy who can help you." With that he walked away.

I couldn't believe what I was hearin'. I wanted to hurt him. I came close to grabbin' my gun and shootin' him in the back. But the truth of his words paralyzed me. I sat there unable to move, thinkin' about what he'd said to me.

Silently I yelled after him, "Who needs you?" and ordered another drink.

In my heart I knew he was right. For a moment I saw that if I stayed in the life I was leadin', I would either spend the rest of my life in prison or die. I had to do somethin' different.

Days went by and I couldn't get Skid's words out of my mind. "You're nothin' but a derelict . . . . you're a danger to me and my family . . . . you need help..." I looked around and thought, "What've I got to lose?" I walked over to the phone, picked up the card Skid had thrown at me, and began dialin' the number.

Things I Think About

- *If you ever hit rock bottom, I hope you have a brother like Skid the Kid who's willin' to put his friendship on the line in order to tell you the truth.*

.

CHAPTER 22

GOIN' STRAIGHT:
Takin'
The Biggest Risk
Of My Life

What I Did After Hittin' Rock Bottom

Ten days after Skid walked out on me, I was sittin' in the waiting room of his yuppie psychologist, wonderin' what I was doin'. I felt uneasy and totally out of place, but I had decided to give this a try and I wasn't gonna back out now.

When my time came, I walked into his office and sat down in a chair facin' him. I told him that my life was messed up: I was laid off from my job at Pabst and was goin' through a divorce. At first things were awkward, but at least he seemed to be really listenin' to what I was tellin' him.

Then he asked what I wanted to accomplish and I told him I wasn't sure — that for the past ten years I had spent most of my time flippin' dope and that I was makin' and losin' more money in one week than he made in a month. Then, slowly, I began to tell him about the crap I was *really* goin' through — with Richie, the busts, the killings, the stings, and losin' my wife and kids.

I hadn't been talkin' very long when I noticed that his attitude had changed. Instead of listenin' to me, he began to smirk and make condescending remarks to me. Suddenly, I realized that this arrogant yuppie doctor didn't believe a word I was tellin' him. So what if I was dressed like a biker and looked like an outlaw? Here I was pourin' my guts out to this sucker, and he didn't believe a word I was tellin' him.

Without takin' my eyes off him, I quietly pulled my 9-millimeter out of its holster, shoved it into his mouth, and asked, "Do you believe *this*, punk?"

His eyes looked like they were gonna pop out of his head and I noticed a wet spot between his legs. I scared the crap out of him, but I had his attention. Immediately he started apologizin' and beggin' for his life.

I told him, "Look, man, I need help, but I won't take your condescendin' b.s. — not here, not ever. Now if you've got some ideas that can help me, I'm ready to listen, but I don't have time for anything else. Don't you ever come at me like that again."

He probably should've called the police for what I'd just done. But, as scared as he was, he recognized that I really was there to get help. And he was man enough or professional enough not to pretend that he could give it to me. Instead, he told me about a friend of his that worked for the Milwaukee Men's Center. He was runnin' a weekly support group for men goin' through divorce, and invited me to give him a call. "You're hurtin' over your divorce, and this way you'll be with other men who are goin' through what you are. You'll be away from the guys that you're with now, and maybe you'll learn somethin' by just bein' with different people." He didn't realize that I was hurtin' from more than the divorce, but it was a start.

As soon as I got home that night, I called the number he gave me. I didn't know it then, but the man who answered would become the best friend I'd ever had in my life.

Bill was the kindest, most respectful man I'd ever talked to. I explained who I was and that I was interested in joining his men's group. He told me that there was a new group forming, so it would be a good time for me to start. When I asked him what I had to do in order to join the group, he told me, "Just come. We meet every Tuesday night. What can I do to support you right now?"

I said, "What can you do to what?" This was very different from what I was used to. I didn't know what he was talkin' about, but I told him I'd come to the next meeting.

The Between Time In Geeksville

That Tuesday I opened the door and walked into a room full of geeks. White upper middle class professional types — the kind of guys I'd tried to stay away from all my life.

Here I was with hair down my back, wearin' two guns — lookin' like a wild man — in a room full of professionals. Stayin' in that room was the hardest thing I'd ever done. Everything in me wanted to bolt for the door and keep on runnin'.

The group began with introductions. Two guys said they were therapists, another one was an architect, and the guy next to me told us he was a dentist. Then it was my turn, and the leader looked at me and asked, "Ron, what do you do?" I answered, "I work at Pabst Brewery." And then somebody else asked me what I did there, and I told them that I delivered beer. I didn't say another word the rest of the night.

I hated it. I couldn't believe that I'd been crazy enough to think that comin' here was gonna be a good idea. I couldn't wait to leave!

That first night I didn't do anything but listen to the other guys talk about what was goin' on in their lives. I watched as the men encouraged one another and supported one another. Nobody laughed. Nobody ridiculed anybody else. By the end of the night, I'd decided that I would give it one more try, and if it didn't get any easier, then I could leave and nobody could say I hadn't tried.

It took me three weeks before I finally risked tellin' the group who I was and what I really did. When I did, I figured that it was as good a time as any, because I thought I'd probably never see these guys again anyway.

I told them that I had been flippin' dope for about ten years, but that I was tryin' to get away from it. I also admitted that I had a $2,000 a week coke habit I was in the process of kickin'.

What blew me away was that they reacted to me the same way they had to everybody else in the group. They encouraged me, cheered me, and supported me, and nobody told me I was wrong. It was incredible. I had never experienced anything like it in my life. I couldn't remember straight people ever treatin' me with dignity before. The funny thing was, they were just as proud to know me as I was to know them.

Those four weeks turned into a year and a half. Durin' that time these geeks became my best friends. They'd call me during the week to see how I was doing, and I began hangin' out with them.

I was learnin' a lot. I was still stuck in a lot of my stuff, and the group really helped me. After a year I was asked to go through a twenty-week training program in order to become a group leader. So I went to the Milwaukee Men's Center, learned how to lead a group, and started running men's groups with a therapist named Jerry Loberg. Now I was in two groups a week.

What had started out as one of the scariest, most painful risks of my life turned out to be the very thing that saved me. But what I want to make sure you understand is that none of it was easy. It wasn't easy lettin' my guard down enough to trust these guys. And I still didn't feel like I belonged, but the fact that the other guys supported me gave me the courage to keep at it.

The hardest thing I ever did was walk away from my old drug dealin' associates and friends. But I knew I had to do somethin' completely different than I had been doin'.

I figured that as long as I didn't care if I lived or died, I had nothin' to lose in tryin' out another life-style. I knew I'd come to the end of my old life — that it wasn't workin' for me anymore — so I figured why not let me try somethin' different?

Exercise — My New Addiction

After I joined the men's group and started gettin' clean, I had more energy than I knew what to do with. I still had plenty of money, and since I was laid off from Pabst, I had a lot of time on my hands.

Now let me clue you in: idleness durin' the "between time" is not good. It gives you too much time to wallow in your stuff. It's too easy to slip back into your old life. I learned that I had to take that energy and channel it in a healthy direction. The times I didn't, I'd get too locked into my old way of thinkin'. In fact, one of the guys in my group suggested that I join the YMCA and start runnin' and exercisin'.

Except for runnin' from squad cars, I hadn't exercised on purpose (outside the hard physical labor I did at the brewery and Coca Cola) since I was in the Army, but I decided I'd give it a try. I started out runnin' a quarter mile. Within two weeks I was up to a mile. I exercised every single day for two hours. I also played a lot of basketball.

I can't tell you how much this helped to keep my mind clear. Exercise became my new drug of choice. I never OD'd on it, but I got in great shape. For the first time since my Army days, I was at 175 lbs. and stayin' there.

The Biggest Risk I Ever Took Was Me

In the support group I led there was a man named Steve, whose favorite pastime seemed to be blamin' his wife and everybody else. Nothing was ever his fault. Now, one thing everybody knew about our group was that we didn't allow any blame and shame. If a guy had to call his wife a bunch of abusive names, he was asked to stop the b.s. or leave. We wanted guys who didn't have to hide behind their wives' problems. Our guys had to be serious about workin' on their own anger and sadness.

Now, Steve was one of these kind of guys that couldn't get past complainin' about his old lady. This went on for months. We kept dealin' with him about it, but he just wasn't gettin' it.

Then one day, he told me about a workshop called "Understanding Yourself and Others" he had decided to do over the weekend. And when he came back to the group the following week, he wasn't stuck on how awful his old lady was — instead he was talkin' about love.

My first thought was, "Oh brother, Steve's gone off the deep end with some cult." I mean, the guy was huggin' people, focusin' on other people, and bein' supportive in ways he had never been before. From then on, Steve became Mr. Positive. He quit focusing on the negative and actually became one of the most positive influences in our group.

Well, this went on for about three or four months, and I finally couldn't stand it any more. I told him I didn't know how he had done it, but I had been a witness to a very big change in his life. A lot of people talk like they've changed for a couple of weeks, then go back to the same-old same-old. But with Steve, I actually watched somebody transform his life.

I had disliked bein' around the man because he was so negative. But after he took the course, I began to enjoy bein' around him. He grew so much that he became one of the leaders of the group.

I started talkin' to him about the course because I saw that he was still spendin' a lot of time with it. Finally, he suggested that I take the course myself. I told him that I didn't need it — that I was already a very positive guy. Compared to my old life, I was on top of the world. I'd been out of my old life for about two years and I was ridin' high.

Then, a few weeks later, Steve and I were sittin' in my kitchen, butcherin' a deer, and I was feelin' real low. Steve looked over at me and said, "You know, Ron, you're scared to take this course."

I asked him, "What did you say?"

He looked at me and said, "I told you you're too chicken to take the course."

I reached over and grabbed him by the neck and told him that if he kept talkin' to me like that, I was gonna lay him out.

He looked at me and said, "Ron, I really care about you, man, but the fact remains that you're scared to take the course."

"I'm not scared of nothin'!" I screamed back at him in my old macho way.

"Well, then take the course. I'll even pay for it."

I told him that I didn't need him to pay for nothin', and he said, "Fine, here are the dates for the next course. Do yourself a favor and just take it." So in the next couple of days I called, made my reservation for the course, and went down and paid the $400.

There are a lot of different types of personal growth workshops. For just about anything you want to learn or experience there's a "how to" workshop out there you can go to. You can learn how to be successful in business, marriage, parenting, golfing, etc. You can face your fears and experience inner courage by doing a fire walk with Tony Robbins or an Outward Bound survival week. There are also intense psychotherapy workshops available to people who are interested in understanding themselves and others better.

The weekend I had signed up for at the Center for Creative Learning turned out to be an intense psychotherapy workshop. There were 12 people enrolled for the weekend, plus one assistant for each person.

The goal of the course was to help us identify the circumstances in our lives which kept us from feelin' good about ourselves and caused us to shut down emotionally.

The painful things which happen to us are like big rocks being tossed into a stream. If enough rocks are thrown in, eventually they form a dam which blocks out everything but the rage.

Those rocks can be anything that hurts: bein' sexually molested, losin' a brother or cousin in a drive-by shooting, bein' abandoned or neglected by parents, havin' an alcoholic or drug addicted parent shootin' or smokin' coke instead of buyin' groceries, or just bein' made to feel like you're stupid.

For me it was the time I had been hit in the eye by the pole.

After the accident I'd been ridiculed and abused for bein' stupid because I couldn't talk. And I began to believe what people said about me, not because it was true, but because I was a kid and I'd been told I was stupid so many times that I began to believe it.

As young kids, we look to other people for clues to tell us who we are. And when other people tell us we're worthless, we usually believe them — sometimes for the rest of our lives.

All of us begin to believe lies about ourselves when we're young: "I'm too fat," "I'm too ugly," "I have to be better then everybody," "I'm no good," etc. Everybody carries around a lot of this garbage and pain from their past.

Real Men Do Cry — Sometimes
It completely blew my mind when the people leading the course took me back to the day before my accident, when I was an innocent five-year-old — before I had been programmed to believe that I was stupid and worthless. It shocked me to remember a time when I wasn't filled with rage and hopelessness.

I actually cried for the first time since I was six or seven years old. I had always been taught that no matter what, guys don't cry. In fact, if I came home hurt and cryin', my dad or my brother Richie would kick my butt for bein' such a sissy.

But now, as a 34-year-old man, tears rolled down my cheeks. I cried for that little boy who had turned his pain and tears into anger, then rage. As I cried I began to let go of the old feelings. I felt lighter and somehow freer inside.

It was then that I realized that I had gone through my whole life thinkin' that I was stupid just because of what other people said to me. Little by little, I stopped caring because of the things that had been said to me. That's how it happens to many of us.

Words can hurt us when we believe what's said — even a little. A lot of times, when we say we don't believe it, in the back of our minds we're thinkin', "What if it is true?" And that becomes enough to make us react, instead of seein' that most of the time people put us down because they're insecure themselves.

What? You Mean Everything's Not About Me?
The course taught me how to recognize other people's b.s. and how not to buy into it anymore. I learned that I didn't have to let other people's words affect me so much. I began to stop personalizing everything, and began realizin' that every time somebody had a bad day, it didn't have to be about me. And I finally realized that I wasn't stupid.

When I began to let go of my anger, I was able to see when other people were hurtin' or just havin' a bad day. I also realized that most of us are more comfortable getting angry than we are expressing the fear or hurt we're really feelin'.

Until that time, if someone said somethin' I didn't like, I'd beat the crap out of them, or I'd get beat up tryin'. But in the course, I began learnin' how to see things from somebody else's point of view.

If somebody talked down to me or dissed me — instead of reactin', I could walk away because it wasn't my stuff. I began to be more relaxed in all of my relationships, because now I was learnin' that I could do and be anything I wanted if I believed in myself and stopped worryin' about what others said about me or how they treated me.

Back to School For A's and B's
Two months after I took this course, I went back to school. This time I had a whole different idea and attitude about myself. Plus, this time, I had people around me who encouraged me and who believed in me, instead of tellin' me to skip class and

go get high. Can you imagine how I felt after all those years believin' that I was stupid, only to end up in college with A's and B's? Go figure.

My experience at the Center for Creative Learning was powerful because I allowed myself to be encouraged and supported in ways I hadn't experienced before. So the next time a course was offered, I went back — this time as a support person.

Every month for over a year I went and participated as an assistant trainer. I then went through a year-long training in the Personal Expression Program. The following two years I was part of a two-year training program for trainers who want to become instructors.

The work I did at the Center turned my life around. For the first time, I learned that I didn't have to feel like a victim — that I didn't have to buy into the negative crap people laid on me. I got to say who I was. I thought about things from a new perspective. I wasn't a victim any more.

Think About It

- *What started out as one of the scariest, most painful risks of my life turned out to be the very thing that saved me.*
- *I had to come to the end of my old life. It wasn't workin' for me anymore, so I figured, why not try somethin' different?*
- *Idle time during the between time is not an easy thing. It gives you too much time to wallow in self-pity and makes it too easy to slip back into your old life.*

CHAPTER 23

The Risk
Pays
Off

The last thing I'd ever want you to think is that the payoff came quick and easy. It never does — not for me, not for anybody. I didn't just wake up one day magically changed into a new person with a new life. And neither will you. If there are things in your life that you wish were different, then you'll have to begin to change how you think. That takes time and hard work.

My New Life: Hey, I'm Not Stupid

The changes in my life have come slowly, over time. After bein' involved in personal growth workshops, I started realizin' that a lot of the old thinking habits I'd developed as a kid hadn't served me very well.

Figurin' out what I wanted to change was only the beginning. Knowin' why I'd felt and acted the way I did in the past helped me see that I didn't have to stay in that old victim role forever. I proved I could change my own life when I went back to school, and I proved it again when I became successful at sellin' machine tools.

For a long time I'd believed that I could never succeed in school because I thought I was stupid. And I thought I couldn't ever be good at sellin' because I was so afraid to talk to people. But now, here were two things I'd failed at in the past, where now I was bein' successful.

For the first time ever, it felt good to be me. There were lots of good things about my new life. I had hope again, and felt I finally had a future worth livin' for. This was big for me 'cuz it had been a long time since I really felt like livin'.

A New High — Help The Other Guy

After I finished a six-month group leadership course at the Milwaukee Men's Center, Jerry asked me to start a new group with him. I felt honored, but it was scary at first. I found out that it's one thing to participate in a group, and a whole other thing to lead one.

I learned a lot from Jerry. Eventually, with experience, I felt confident enough to run the group — whether Jerry was there or not. It was fun to encourage and support other people. There's nothin' like the high you get when you help others. Plus, I was gettin' lots of support from everyone around me.

But believe me, everything wasn't easy. I had to take things one day at a time. After all, I wasn't used to feelin' this good, and it was hard to trust it. It was kinda like I'd moved to a whole new country where I didn't know anybody, and they didn't know me. Everything was new to me. There were lots of days when the pull of the old familiar way of life and thinkin' was strong.

The truth is, I did go back a few times and get high with my old buddies. But each time I slipped it was harder to stay. It never took me long to remember why I had left that life in the first place. When this happened, I didn't use it as an excuse to quit tryin'. I'd call one of my new buddies and we'd talk it out, and I'd keep on goin'.

I Learned What It's Like To Be Loved

When I first started opening up with my heart it was very scary, because I hadn't done it in years. I had rage and anger down pat, but this was a whole new thing for me. I found out the more I opened up with my heart, the easier it became.

I'd been workin' with the Center for Creative Learning for about two years, and had been divorced about four, when I met the woman who would become my second wife, my business partner, and my teacher. She also became my biggest cheerleader. We began a relationship where there was honesty, communication, and real support. For the first time in my life, my best friend was a woman.

I hadn't ever met anyone who came from a place of love and acceptance in the way she does. This was somethin' completely new to me. I was learnin' how to have a relationship where there was real give and take.

For a long time Terri had been focused on the spiritual aspects of life. She was totally committed to learnin' about where she was stuck so she could continue to grow. She taught me how to speak from my heart instead of just from my head, and to trust my gut and intuition.

A Legal Business Of Our Own

Terri and I were together for only a year when we decided to get married. At the time I was sellin' machine tools on the international market. I was makin' good money, but I wasn't happy workin' for somebody else. I wanted my own company. Terri wanted to go into the import business — bringin' brass and other items into the United States from India — so we began lookin' at different possibilities.

Spirit Bear Of The North

Then one of those things happened which a lot of people consider to be a coincidence. Terri and I were at a weekend work-shop, and someone played a tape called "You Are All You Need To Be" — a powerful, healing song about self-respect, confidence, and belief in yourself. Terri was deeply affected by the song and decided that she would buy it for all of our friends.

The next day she called the company and found out they sold a talking and singing bear named Spinoza. The tape she wanted to buy was only one in a series they sold. She ordered just about everything. A few days later, the bear and tapes arrived at our house. From then on, our lives were never the same.

Terri had a vision that she was supposed to work with this bear. She wasn't sure how or in what way, but she was sure that she was supposed to work with the company.

So Terri went to Minnesota to meet with the women who owned the company. Our original idea was for her to talk to them about her handlin' a sales territory. She'd market the bear, and I'd continue to sell machine tools. It sounded like a great plan.

What she got was the biggest surprise of her life. They wanted to sell her the whole company. They were creators, not businesswomen, and they hated the business aspects of the company. But because Spinoza was more than just another teddy bear, they weren't willin' to sell him and the company to just anybody. They could see that Terri had been given a special vision of the bear's mission, so they wanted *her* to take over the company.

When I found out that we had a chance to own the entire company, I got interested. Although Terri always saw the bear from a spiritual and healing point of view, it took me a little longer to grasp what a huge impact the bear could have in the lives of people.

In the beginning I thought of him only as a money-maker. But eventually, I began to realize that Spinoza could help a lot of people. I also realized that things might have been different for me if I'd heard the messages of Spinoza when I lost my ability to talk. Most people never hear that they're OK, that they're good enough just the way they are. Hearin' him tell me I was good enough might have made a big difference for me when I was a kid, and I figured it could help other people, too.

You're Always Good Enough

Spinoza's messages are: "You are special," "you are always good enough," and "there is hope for tomorrow." I didn't see it at the time, but it was as though everything Terri and I had been through in our lives had prepared us for this moment. Here we were being given an opportunity to own a business which would allow us to share the new lessons I'd spent the past three years learnin'.

It took us eight years, but we built the company from a home based business to a multimillion dollar company. We've made a lot of mistakes and paid a lot of dues. Nothin' about ownin' this company has been easy. But Spinoza has been an incredible learnin' experience for me.

Over the years I've had lots of struggles and ups and downs, and many times I felt like just sayin'," I quit." But I gotta tell ya, despite all the hassles, and hardships, workin' with Spinoza has changed me in ways I never imagined when I first got involved with the company. The new concepts and spiritual principles I'd been learnin' quit bein' ideas and became my way of life. Bein' of service to others was no longer just a nice thought. Our entire reason for bein' in business was to be of service to others — not just ourselves.

I'll tell you this: If anybody would've told me twelve years ago that I'd go from makin' over $100,000 sellin' machine tools to makin' $24,000 that first year sellin' a talkin' teddy bear I'd have told them they were out of their minds! And you know what else? Ten years ago I didn't know that I'd love workin' with teddy bears so much. I'd have made a lot more money if I'd stayed in the machine tool business, but I wouldn't have been livin' out my life purpose, and I'd have missed out on a lot.

Lessons I Learned In The Street
That Helped Me Succeed In Business
Never give up.

Most people don't succeed the first time they try somethin'. For this reason, if you want to be successful, you can't let failure stop you.

When I was a kid, my brother Richie taught me a lesson I would use throughout my whole life — the importance of not wimpin' out. He always told me that in a fight — just like in all of life — you never give up until you've won, or used up your last ounce of strength tryin'. I didn't know it at the time, but I was learnin' the importance of persistence — to keep on tryin' no matter what the road-blocks may seem to be. I won a lot of fights simply because I refused to give up; and the times I lost, I gained the other guy's respect because I wouldn't quit.

Like lots of other people, I've accomplished some of my most important achievements simply because I wasn't willin' to give up just because somethin' was hard or somebody told me it was a dumb idea.

I can't tell you how many times I've fallen flat on my face. But I always get back up, dust off my knees, and keep on tryin'.

Experts claim that most businesses fail in the first year for one of three reasons: they don't have enough money, they have poor marketing, or the owners lack persistence. People just give up too soon. Listen, for every 10 new ideas I try in my business, nine of them fail. But that tenth idea is usually a killer, and sometimes it takes off in a big way.

Look, I know I've said this before. In fact, you're probably gettin' sick of hearin' about it. I don't care if it bores you, the important thing to me is that you take it in: Real life is about trial and error! You try somethin', if it doesn't work, you don't quit, you modifiy the idea or go on and try somethin' else. Just don't give up. Eventually you're gonna get it right.

Old Colonel Sanders, the founder of Kentucky Fried Chicken, was turned down 600 times before he finally figured out how to sell his idea for a chicken take-out store. Can you even imagine? If he had quit the 599th time, you and I wouldn't know that his idea really was "finger lickin' good."

Thomas Edison, the inventor of the light bulb, tried over a thousand times before he finally got it right. In the process, he used up all his money and had to get a bank loan to finish his project. When the banker asked Edison why he should loan him money for a project that had already failed a thousand times, Edison replied: "Think of it this way. I've already learned a thousand ways not to invent a light bulb, so I'm a thousand times closer to gettin' it right." He didn't think of all his failures as reasons to quit. Instead, he saw them as valuable lessons that had helped him get closer to the right answer.

There've been plenty of times when it would have been much easier for me to walk away from a relationship or a business deal, instead of hangin' in there and makin' it work. But I didn't. And I can't tell you how glad I am that I didn't.

Don't get me wrong. There are times when you don't have any choice but to quit — at least for a while. But you'll know those times when you see them. It's like the song says: "You gotta know when to hold 'em, know when to fold 'em, and know when to walk away."

But most of us don't fail because we hang in there too long. Most of us fail because we quit before we ever really get started. So what if you make some mistakes along the way? The real losers in life are the chumps who sit on the side-lines, too afraid to try. If you think some people are born winners, then you've been watchin' too much television.

The Value Of Other People
Remember the old saying, "What goes around, comes around"? This couldn't be truer than in business. The bottom line in business is knowin' people, likin' people, and servin' people by hookin' them up with one another.

When I was on the street I fine-tuned my ability to work with other people to get what I wanted. I learned that things work best when you create win-win situations, when there's real give and take. Whether it's on the street or in the straight business world, relationships break down if only a couple of people are doin' all the giving and everybody else is doin' the taking. That's why I always treated my people with respect and dignity. I tried my hardest to make sure that people enjoyed doin' business with me.

When I was in the dope business, I only dealt in a limited number of products. People came to me to buy marijuana or coke. But I knew people in all kinds of businesses, so if somebody wanted heroin, or a lady for the night, or a hot car or stereo, I could always put them in touch with the right people.

If I sent a person to somebody, they always knew they'd get a good deal and didn't have to be afraid of bein' screwed. These business owners did the same for me. They'd come to me when they wanted somethin', and they'd send their people to me.

In the straight world, the people who do well in sales enjoy people, know how to network, and are willin' to go the extra mile for a customer. They love what they're doin'. I'm a good networker because I love people and I enjoy helping people just for the sake of helping them. I don't *require* somethin' in return for my help. But you know what? I always get back as much or more than I give.

Goin' The Extra Mile

It's the extra two feet you go that add 80% of the success. Everybody wants the best they can buy for the money. If you provide a quality service or product, people are going to remember you and come back again. Whether you're in business out on the street or in business on Main Street, USA, good quality and good service will take you a long way.

When I was buildin' up my marijuana business, I learned that it was the little extras that you do for people that keep them coming back. There were lots of guys out there selling pot, but I was the only one who included a box of matches and rollin' papers. When I was in the cocaine business, I'd give people a razor, a small mirror, and a sterling silver straw if they bought an ounce from me. My customers went nuts. They loved that they didn't have to wait to get home to do a bump or a line.

When I quit sellin' dope, I carried this principle over into my own company. Competition is stiff. No matter what business you're in, poor quality and bad service never made anyone successful. You might get away with it for a little while, but in the long run you'll wind up a loser.

You Are Your Word

Bein' a stand-up guy is important, no matter who you are. Everybody knows that if you can't be trusted, you're gonna end up buyin' a whole lot of trouble for yourself. Every day somebody ends up in the hospital or dies on the street because they didn't keep their word.

A word of warning: there probably are as many liars and cheaters doin' business in the straight world as there are in the street. There might even be more. Why am I mentioning this? Because I want to make it clear that people are people, and it doesn't matter where you are, you're gonna run into some dogs.

Doin' business on the street, I learned how important it is to establish trusting relationships with people. Ya gotta be good at readin' people and situations.

Believe it or not, the same is true in the straight business world. The difference is, in the straight world you're playin' for different stakes. My ability to develop trusting relationships has made it possible for Spinoza to get and keep good investors and suppliers.

Trust Goes Farther Than Money

When we first started out in the company, we didn't have a whole lot of cash for inventory. Through my networking, I was able to locate an outstanding supplier who was willin' to put his own money on the line, simply because he believed in the project and the fact that he had learned that he could trust us to honor our commitments. We didn't let him down, and the relationship turned into a profitable one for both of us.

You might make a quick score by rippin' somebody off — on the street or in the straight world. But you're gonna pay a high price if you do. Believe me when I tell you that if you're a man of your word, and people know that they can trust you, it won't matter where you do business. In the long run, havin' a reputation for keepin' your word will be like money in the bank.

Think About It

- *Life changes are never easy — they come one day at a time.*
- *Losers are the chumps who sit along the sidelines afraid to try new things in life.*
- *Most people aren't successful the first few times they do something. For this reason, you can't let failure stop you if you want to be successful.*
- *Networking is the art of helpin' other people get what they want or need by hookin' them up with other people's wants and needs.*
- *In the long run, havin' a reputation for keepin' your word is like money in the bank.*

PART SIX:

Secrets of My Real Success

CHAPTER 24

Players
Who've Made It

Refusin' To Get Stuck Halfway

Ever hear the saying, "The road to hell is paved with good intentions"? Well, actually, it's littered with the bodies of the people who had all those good intentions. A lot of 'em crashed and burned 'cuz they didn't know it takes more than good intentions to make it through the between time. The good news is: you don't have to be one of 'em.

Yeah, it's hard to get away from friends and the old ways of thinkin' and doin' things. It's real hard, but not impossible. Just ask an old alcoholic how many excuses he's gone through — or an old junkie how many reasons he's got to get high. We're geniuses when it comes to polishin' up the same old sorry excuses. The thing is, the bottom line in most excuses is usually "I can't help it" or "I don't have no choice."

I've Failed More Times Than You

Look, I'm not sayin' you'll never blow it. There'll be times when you will. Along the way, I've blown it, too. I've had my share of failures. So if you think you're gonna make it through the between time without ever blowin' it, think again, man. If you're still breathin' you're gonna blow it once in a while.

But brother, if you find yourself goin' in the wrong direction — turn around! You do have a choice.

As my friend LeRoy "Sonny" Jackson says, " You can change your thoughts like you change the gears in a car — from reverse to forward." Just decide which direction you wanna go in.

What makes me so sure that you can get out of that rut you call a life, and move onto better things? Just one thing: the thousands of suckers just like me who've already made it through the between time. If we can make it through, so can you. If I can get my act together, anybody can.

Three Ways To Turn Your Life Around:

1. Make the choice to believe in yourself.
2. Set goals: Where do ya wanna end up?
3. Surround yourself with people who'll
   help you along the way.

How They Made It
Here are some real people — people just like me — who've made it through the between time and are gettin' their lives together.

Ronnie W.
Minnesota
Ex-Con, Ex-Scam Artist, and Ex-Junkie
I've spent a total of 12 years of my life in the penitentiary. I started out hustling when I was in elementary school. I was good at it. It was easy, and it kept nice clothes on my back and

spending money in my pocket. I started drinking in grade school. In junior high, I smoked weed and drank. I was in high school in the sixties, and for a while I got into the Jimmy Hendrix, LSD psychedelic trip.

When I was in high school, one of my brothers-in-law recognized my potential and turned me on to selling fake jewelry. We got real tight. He was my teacher, and my best friend. For a kid my age it was a great hustle, and by the time I was 19 I was able to buy my first Cadillac.

Around this time my friend got into dealing heroin, and he cut me out of the business end of his life. I didn't understand it, and our relationship was never the same after that. I had temporarily lost my jewelry connection, and decided to start doing armed robberies. I never was very good at it, and there wasn't much money in it. Eventually I got busted and got 0-20 on an armed robbery charge. I ended up doing two years at a hard labor camp.

While I was there I took an accounting course. When I got out I got a job with Cargill as a junior accountant trainee.

This was the early seventies, and I had moved into an apartment building filled with players — everybody thought they were Super Fly. Naturally, I thought I had to keep up with the game, and since my little salary at Cargill wasn't enough to allow me to live in the style I wanted, I developed a new bank scam. By this time, I was addicted to heroin and life in the fast lane.

In 1975 I was busted by the Bunco Squad and got 0-10 for confidence crimes. This time I spent 18 months in Stillwater Prison. When I got out I went right back to hustling and heroin.

For the next few years I was in and out of treatment programs and prison. The only thing I seemed to learn was how to talk the talk. I wasn't letting anything past my head. It all just became part of the game I was playing with myself.

In 1979 I met and married my wife, and for the next ten years I lived the straight life. I cleaned my life up and started selling insurance. I was a good husband, a good father, a good provider.

Then in 1988 I started hanging out with some of my old high school friends. I started noticing that they seemed to be really doing well. I got curious, and they finally let me know that they were dealing coke and that, if I wanted in, they'd hook me up.

My friend turned over nine ounces of coke to me to flip for him. Well, that was a big mistake. I tasted that coke, and by the time I was done, it became evident to me that I was still too much of an addict to handle dealing. One thing lead to another, and I was back out there hustling again.

Then in 1990 I got a big break. I had met Sharif Willis when I was in the joint, and he hooked me up with a good managerial job at the Minnesota Department of Transportation. Unfortunately, cocaine was still running my life. Instead of playing it straight, I turned my job into an opportunity to develop a major credit card scam. This time I was busted by the United States Secret Service and the FBI. Believe me, the Feds don't like it when you start messing with the money system.

The biggest break I've ever gotten was getting into treatment at Eden House. The biggest break I've ever given myself was to really start taking a hard look at myself this time. I knew I had to stop all the b.s., and really face myself. No more excuses. This time it wasn't about playing the game — it was about my life. I had to look at who I really am, and what I'm about. I had to look at my values, and my thinking processes — what is really important in my life.

I've recently gotten out of prison and have started rebuilding my life. This time I have a different attitude and outlook on life. I know that my value as a man cannot be equated with my material possessions. My value, and the quality of my life, don't originate out in the streets, they come from within me.

You know, too often we take our freedom for granted until it's snatched away as a result of doing some stupid, senseless deed. You don't have to lose your freedom to realize how valuable it is. All you have to do is heed our stories. Cause man, there's no worse feeling in the world than hearing the steel cell doors slam behind you as you enter jail — not knowing if you'll ever make it back to your home or the hood to be with your people.

Skid The Kid
Arizona
Ex-Drug User and Dope Dealer
I got into the business because I saw the kind of money that could be made. I had just been through a divorce, and I was looking for ways to get my life back together again.

For a while it was exciting to be the man; to walk into a place and be the one everybody wanted to see. The money and the partying were great. I thought I had little to lose, and a whole lot to gain. So I began to live two lives. I kept my straight life with my family and friends separate from the life I was living in the streets.

At first, it seemed easy to keep it all under control. But then things began to change. I started using up more and more of my profits, and I saw more and more of my buddies getting busted or killed. By this time I had remarried, and it was getting harder to keep things from my wife. Family was the most important thing in my life, and there was no way I wanted to risk losing my wife.

One night I was at home watching television, and I happened

to flip the channel past a program where a preacher was telling cocaine users and dealers that they could be free from their old life, and have a new life. I'm not sure what happened. The only thing I can say is that the holy spirit came over me, and I realized that preacher meant me.

That night I made my final decision to get out of the life, but it took me months before I had collected all my money, and straightened things out enough so that I could actually walk away.

I got a lot of pressure from my supplier not to quit. We'd been good friends a long time, and it wasn't easy just to walk away, But I saw that his life was more out of control than mine, and I wasn't willing to risk dying, losing my family or having to spend some hard time in jail.

It was my wife, my spiritual beliefs and getting away from my old friends that helped me the most. It wasn't easy rebuilding a trusting relationship with my wife, but time and God have done a lot to heal both of us.

Billy
Georgia
Ex-Con, Ex-Drug Trafficker

I started smokin' dope when I was 14 and dealin' dope when I was 17. I started out flippin' small amounts, but when I saw the kind of money I could really make I got into it full time. By the time I was 20 I was bringin' millions of dollars worth of marijuana into the country — at age 25 I was bringin' in millions of dollars worth of cocaine. I was hooked up with people from LA to south Florida. For a while it was a great life. One big party.

You may think this is funny, but now, lookin' back, it isn't easy for me to think about my life back then — much less talk about it. I'm not proud of the things I've done to people for the sake of money.

When I was 29 the DEA and IRS got me, and I spent a long time as a guest of the federal government. I spent years bein' shuttled from one federal joint to another. Believe me, this was no vacation.

When I walked away from the joint this last time, I made up my mind that I was never goin' back.

It hasn't been easy goin' through the between time. Have you heard the old sayin', "You can take the man out of the country, but you can't take the country out of the man?" Well, it's a lot like that with prison life. When you walk out through the gates you bring the prison with you. It's hard to get rid of those old attitudes and ways.

I'm 40 years old and I'm startin' life all over. I've been lucky because I've met some good people who've given me a lot of support. I'd have to say that the biggest change in me is my desire to simplify my life. I don't place the same value on money and material things that I used to.

And for the first time in my life I'm opening up to the possibility of the spiritual aspects of life. I'm in a real learnin' mode. I read everything I can get my hands on. I've met some real special people who've made me reconsider the existence of a true spiritual reality. I'm excited about the spiritual changes that are happenin' in my life.

I know I still have a long ways to go, but the old life holds no glamour or interest for me anymore. I'm looking ahead — not back.

LeRoy "Sonny" Jackson
Ex-Gang Leader
Minnesota
I became involved with gangs in the late 1950's and early 60s. I started usin' drugs in the 50s and ended up in prison. When

I got out in 1965, I went to Chicago, and connected up with a couple of the local brothers. They said they liked my style — that I had a lot to contribute to the community and wanted me to hook up with them. What they were layin' out was real intriguing. They made it sound like we'd be workin' together to make conditions better in the African American community.

What we put together became the Black "P" Stone Nation.

I became a charter member of the Main 21, who mapped out the details of how the organization was gonna run. In the beginnin,' our goal was to work with the young kids: to get 'em off the street and into school. We were gonna' be lookin' out for the kids, and wanted to stop the crossfire killin' — to stop kids killin' kids.

Drugs were out. Absolutely no use of drugs. In fact, if a member got caught usin' he'd be punished by havin' to enter the circle of the Main 21, and he'd get beat, or shot in the leg — somethin' to let him know that usin' drugs was simply out of the question.

Then about six months after bein' a part of this, things began to change. Suddenly, I learned that it was OK to *sell* drugs, we just weren't supposed to use 'em. At this point we began to recruit the young African American kids on the fringes of the gang. These kids really needed somebody they could look up to and respect, because for most of them their home life was nothin'. A lot of their mothers were drug addicts and their daddies were goin' back and forth to jail. So they were good recruits.

Now I'm sittin' back watchin' these things happen, and listenin' to how we were supposedly sellin' drugs not to harm the community, but to raise money in order to make the community better. There were a few guys who'd occasionally give $50 or $100 to somebody in the neighborhood, but this was nothin' compared to the money that was bein' made.

I watched this goin' down for years, and finally I went to the leadership and said, "Look, man, this ain't the way this thing should be done." We talked, but he made it sound OK. You know, the end justifying the means, and all that.

After a certain period of time seein' these young brothers gettin' busted for drugs, goin' to court, and bein' put right back out on the streets; and watchin' how they'd be beat up if they didn't bring the money back right — it kinda changed my opinion about what the whole thing was about. So I split to St. Louis. But while I was there I started chippin' again, got busted and was sent back to the penitentiary.

The next bit I did was in Statesville, Indiana, and that's where I met one of the leaders of the Gangster Disciples. We started talkin', and his rap was the same thing I heard in Chicago about how we got to build, and that GD don't stand for Gangster Disciples, it stands for Growth and Development — dang, this sounded good. So I asked him, "Growth and development of what?" And he said growth and development of the youth and growth and development of our community.

Now every gang leader was usin' this rap about "let's get the community together," while they were steady tearin' the community down with the drugs and the shootin'.

Then in the mid 60s things were gettin' pretty hot on the streets, so when Richard Nixon was elected president he invited one of our leaders to his inauguration. Now, he didn't want to go so he sent a couple other guys. He asked me to go, but I told him I couldn't make it, 'cuz I didn't want to go any more than he did.

Anyway, these guys got people in Washington thinkin' that we were all about doin' great things for our community, so the government came up with two million dollars for the gang youth organization. The money was meant for the Woodlawn community, and everybody was thinkin' that this was gonna go to build new housing and clean up the community. We'd be able to get things done.

It turned out that some of the brothers decided that since the government had given the money to *us*, we were gonna use some of it for ourselves. People started buyin' diamond rings and drivin' new Cadillacs. All of a sudden, everybody started gettin' busted for what they called "misappropriatin' funds." A whole lot of people went to jail behind this.

By this time I had begun to change my belief system, and in 1968, after I got out of the penitentiary, I started workin' as security for Elijah Mohammed, and got real close to Malcolm and Mr. Mohammed and the Black Muslim family.

In 1984 I met my wife, and that's when I began to make some serious changes. I stopped goin' out on the street, and started really workin' with the community. I began helpin' the old people livin' on my block to clean things up. I knew that I was gonna have to get out of the life, otherwise I'd end up dead or spendin' the rest of my life in the penitentiary.

Some of the guys didn't want to let me out. But gettin' out of gangs ain't no big issue. The real issue is bein' sincere about gettin' out. You gotta mean that you really want out. And you don't go to the guys on the bottom — you go straight to the top, to the leader, to present your case. You let him know, not that you want to get out, but that you're out, you're through.

Even though I had the support of my wife and family, I still had a lot of failures along the way. In 1989 I began chippin' again with the drugs, and went back to the penitentiary. But this time I was serious about makin' the total change.

I learned to be conscious of when my thoughts were takin' me off onto a course that wasn't good, and I'd tell myself, 'stop' — I was goin' the wrong way, and if I continued to follow this course I was gonna really have problems.

My spiritual beliefs in Islam played a very strong part in bringing about the permanent changes in my life. I engrossed myself in my religious beliefs to the point that they became not just good ideas, but my true way of life. I engrossed myself in a completely different way of thinkin' and livin'.

Today there's nothin' enticing to me about the old ways. Not the power, not the prestige, not the money. Money, you understand, is the major attraction of the game. Diamond rings, gold chains around your neck and all that kind of stuff. This is what attracts — it's one of the baits. The government used two million dollars as a bait and trap, and they sent a lot of people to jail for a lot of years.

There's nothin' wrong with money. Everybody needs money to live, but don't get so caught up in the money that you stab yourself or your brother in the back. Don't get so caught up in the money that you don't have no principles about life.

Don't be nobody's chump. Investigate everything you hear from the older leaders. How much truth is in what they're sayin'? Use your own mind.

The main thing that got me over was learnin' to be conscious and aware of where my thoughts were leadin' me. I learned that I could change my thoughts just like I change the gears in a car — from reverse to forward. Since I learned that I have the power to change my own thoughts, I have created the life-style I want. I'm a family man and I have a place where I really belong.

Lynn
Colorado
Ex-Drug User and Small Time Dealer

I'd made the decision to leave the life a whole year before I physically walked away. I probably could have left sooner, but I'd convinced myself that there were too many loose ends I had to take care of before I actually walked. Besides, in my mind, I was givin' up everything: my reputation, my home, my friends, my man.

The truth is, I was walkin' away from a self-destructive life filled with b.s., paranoia, and pain. I didn't like the woman who looked back at me every morning. I was tired, and I wanted more out of life than death or doin' time.

If I had known how hard the transition was going to be, I might not have had the courage to get out when I did. I didn't realize that moving from the drug world into the straight world was going to be like moving to a new country where I didn't even know how to speak the language.

I felt like I had entered the twilight zone. I was scared and lonely. The only thing that kept me going those first few months was the fact that I had moved out of state, and none of my old friends knew where I was. Besides, I had burned all my bridges behind me so I couldn't go back if I wanted to. When I left I had made a lot of people mad, and I was scared I'd be killed — so there was no goin' back. I *had* to learn how to survive in this new world — I hadn't left myself any other options.

The first thing I had to learn was not to take myself so seriously. I had to lighten up. Physical exercise and spending time out in nature gradually helped me develop an inner calm I had never experienced .

I began meeting people who had an inner spiritual dimension that gave things deep meaning and purpose. I was intrigued by the peace that seemed to fill their lives. I began studying everything I could get my hands on. I learned about unconditional love, and forgiveness, and trusting the Creator of the universe as the source and provider of all my needs.

That was twenty-four years ago. Looking back, I realize that the most important thing I've done for myself has been to change how I see myself, others, and the world I live in.

I'm Native American, but most of my family live according to the values of the dominant European culture, so as a child, I was never taught to value the old ways.

Over time, I've gradually learned that as I travel the sacred circle of life I am presented with lessons that can help me understand who I am and how I am connected with the Creator and all of creation. I'm learning how to walk in balance and harmony and practice the law of right relationship. These lessons are helping me come into a deeper understanding of myself and my true purpose as I walk my path.

Recently, somebody asked me if there was anything I miss about the old days. I didn't even have to think about it. The answer is — nothing. Today I have a nice home, two beautiful children, a career as a psychiatric nurse, and an extended family that is nurturing and supportive. I have learned how to value my native heritage, and be at peace with who I really am.

You Can Let Go Of The Past

Do you get it? Can you hear what we're sayin'? Can you see that even though our backgrounds and the details of our stories are all different, all of us who made it through the between time have some basic things in common?

Originally we all believed that money would fix everything that was wrong with our lives. After we got money, greed took over:

Players Who've Made It

we still hated ourselves, and were dissatisfied with our lives. In fact, most of us were more miserable than ever. Fast money had not made our lives better or easier; it had complicated them.

Once we decided to regain control of our lives, most of us who've made it through the between time have used similar principles of success. We learned to take responsibility for our own thoughts and actions. We learned how to change how we think about ourselves, our possibilities, and the world around us. Each of us was able to identify harmful decisions and beliefs from early in our lives — decisions and beliefs that kept us stuck in the old life. We decided that fast money just wasn't worth the price we had to pay when we did the crime. There had to be more to life than what fast money could buy.

Things To Think About

- *If you find yourself goin' in the wrong direction — simply turn around.*
- *There's no worse feelin' in the world than hearin' the steel cell doors slam behind you as you enter jail — not knowin' if you'll ever make it back to your home or the hood to be with your people.*
- *Money's the bait — the major attraction of the game. There's nothin' wrong with money, just don't get so caught up in money that you're willin' to stab yourself or your brother in the back.*
- *Don't be nobody's chump.*
- *Be aware of where your thoughts are leadin' you. Remember, you can change your thoughts just like you change the gears in a car — from reverse to forward.*

CHAPTER 25

What To Do When You're Between Two Worlds

Everything You Need Is Already Inside You

Hold on! Before you go rollin' your eyes and tunin' me out! This is not where I start tryin' to sell you my special brand of spirituality. I'm not tryin' to sell you anything. But it wouldn't be honest for me to leave out how my spiritual beliefs have helped me over the past ten years.

My spiritual beliefs give my life meaning and help me focus on the big picture instead of just the drama of right now. They've helped me redefine myself, and how I relate to the world. And most importantly, they've given me the courage to keep on goin' when I just wanted to say, "forget it."

Growin' up, I always figured that anything spiritual had to do with goin' to church, or bein' religious. And since church was just another place where I got in trouble and was made to feel I didn't fit in, spirituality wasn't exactly somethin' that I cared much about.

I *sure* couldn't see how it had anything to do with success or real life. Oh, I think I believed in God, but I pretty much figured that if He didn't bother me, I wouldn't bother Him. I mean, after all, I had things to do and places to go. I was afraid that if I knew more about God, I'd have to look at myself. And then maybe I wouldn't want to sell dope or run in the fast lane. I might even have to start thinkin' about straightenin' out my life, and I didn't know how to do that. It was just too much for me to think about.

After I started spendin' time at the Center for Creative Learning, I began meetin' people who talked about spirituality in ways I'd never heard before. At first I thought they were nuts, but when I got to know them, I saw that they had somethin' in their lives I didn't have in mine. I learned that spirituality is a personal experience, and that it means different things to different people.

They talked about things like hope, love, truth, and forgiveness as powerful tools for freedom, personal power, and self-respect. It wasn't easy for me to relate to these things, because all my life I'd lived with hate, lies, bitterness and revenge.

I actually got to know people who took responsibility for the things they thought and the things they did. Their spirituality was a way of life, not just somethin' they talked about one day a week. I had never met people like this before.

I decided to check things out for myself and started readin' everything I could get my hands on. It took a while, but I finally began to open up to the possibilities of the spiritual realm.

The Law of Cause And Effect — Everything You Do, Good and Bad, Comes Back To You

Gradually I learned about the physical and spiritual laws that govern the way we live. One of the most powerful is the law of cause and effect. Hindus and Buddhists call this karma. Christians refer to it as reaping what we sow. Moses, described it as an eye for an eye and a tooth for a tooth. Moslems talk about Kismet, a person's lot in life.

These are all different ways of describing the universal law of harmony and balance, which makes sure that every cause set in motion will sometime in the future bring about its proper effect. This means that whatever we do will come back to us — maybe not today or tomorrow, but somewhere down the line.

Everything we do — good or bad — returns to us like a boomerang. Sooner or later, what we put out is what we get back.

When our actions bring happiness and success to others, the eventual fruit of our karma is happiness and success. But if our actions are violent and destructive, our karma becomes violence and destruction. It's like the old saying, "He who lives by the sword dies by the sword."

It didn't take me long to see how this works. All I had to do was look around me. I can tell you one thing, when I think about all the negative karma I've created in my life, it motivates me to be more careful about the choices I make. 'Cuz, man, all the stuff I pulled on people, all the things I thought I got away with, have brought me nothin' but trouble and pain.

Native American spiritual traditions combined with certain Eastern philosophies helped me make it through the between time.

Look, I'm not a guru, or a preacher, or a priest, or a spiritual teacher. So I'm not tryin' to tell you that you have to follow any certain spiritual tradition or that one tradition is more right than the other. If you've read the stories in chapter twenty-three, you already know that religious and spiritual beliefs were important to the rebuilding of most of these people's lives. And everyone had the same beliefs.

My hope is that if you do have a religious or spiritual belief that works for you, then you'll draw strength from it. If you don't have a dynamic spiritual practice, or church group, then I encourage you to find one that feels right to you.

I don't know what's best for you. But *you* will, if you look for it.

It's Easy To Get a New Life —
Keepin' It Is Another Thing
There are three big difficulties faced when startin' a new life:

Procrastination
You know, I made the decision to quit gettin' high and stop sellin' dope every night for years. I'd come home ripped and exhausted, and I'd think, "This is the last time I'm ever gonna get like this." But then tomorrow would come, and before I knew it I'd be right back out there, relivin' the nightmare.

How many times have you seen someone you know try to stop smokin', or lose weight, or quit drinkin'? The thing is, it's not enough just to say you're gonna have a new life, 'cuz there's always a good reason to put it off. We're great at puttin' things off: "I'm gonna start tomorrow, or next week, or next month." But guess what! There is no tomorrow or next week. There's only today. Today is the day to begin. So throw out all your old excuses and just do it.

Other people
Ask anybody who's ever followed their own dreams, and they'll tell you they got the most negative comments from their friends and family. This isn't always true, but it's true most of the time. Some people have very supportive families, but most people don't. The thing is, don't expect your old buddies to cheer you on. Misery loves company. Besides, if you succeed, how's that gonna make them look? People love to bring you down because they don't wanna see you go off and leave them behind. Then it'll be that much harder for them to use their old tired

excuses.

Fear of change
All of us can get caught in this trap. It's human nature to fear change. Or is it? Actually, what we call the fear of change is usually unfounded fear of the unknown. You know I'm tellin' you the truth. How many guys do you know who stayed in jobs they hated because they didn't know where they'd find another job if they quit? How many couples do you know who stayed together long after the relationship went sour just because they were afraid of the unknown? Most people feel that no matter how bad things are today, at least they're in familiar territory, and that's got to be better than not knowin' what's out there waitin' for us.

Why is it we figure the unknown is always gonna be worse than what we're doin' now? Why don't we automatically believe the unknown is filled with exciting possibilities that are out there just waitin' for us to take the first steps?

The truth is, a lot of times we use the fear of change and the unknown to justify our secret belief that we really don't deserve better than what we've got.

New Skills To Keep You On Track
Powerful results from usin' little magic cards.

Durin' my early days in the between time, I realized that I was never gonna make it unless I did somethin' to change my thinkin'. A friend told me that she'd been writin' the new thoughts she wanted on little cards. Mostly she wrote down positive thoughts she wanted to have about herself so she could believe she was good enough. She called 'em affirmation cards, and she'd gotten some powerful results from usin' 'em.

It sounded pretty dumb to me, but I figured that I had nothin' to lose, so I got a bunch of little cards and wrote out the new thoughts I wanted.

I put these magic little cards all over my house. I taped them to my bathroom mirror, to my walls, to my phone. I carried them with me wherever I went and looked at them when I had a few minutes waitin' in line at the post office or at a stoplight. I even made tapes of these new affirmations and played them in my car and at night before I went to bed.

This may sound stupid to you, but man, let me tell you, it works! Not overnight, but over weeks and months. It works because it's a way to commit yourself to reprogramming that computer you call your mind every single day.

The success I've experienced in business, in relationships, and in my spiritual life didn't come about because I read a few affirmation cards a couple times a week. My successes have resulted from conditioning myself *every day* to be the best I can be, and to give my best no matter what I'm doin'.

Garbage In, Garbage Out
This is true about computers and it's true about your mind. If you fill your mind with old negative thoughts, and keep playin' those thoughts over and over, you'll have a much harder time changin' the direction of your life. That's because what we think and how we feel determine our actions. If you think like a loser, you're gonna act like a loser.

When I first started usin' the cards, I just couldn't buy that they'd work — but I stayed with it.

And, to my surprise, they did start to work after a couple months. Think about it. I'd spent 34 years allowin' myself to be programmed that I was stupid. I was programmed by my experience, my thoughts, and what people said about me. So it took a lot more than just repeatin' a couple times, *"I am intelligent*

and have what it takes to succeed in school." I had to repro-
gram my thoughts. It took a long time, but I finally made it.
And I have proof that I made it: I graduated from college with
a 3.4 grade point average.

Free Your Butt and Your Mind Will Follow
OK, I just said that positive thoughts promote positive actions.
Well, get this! The opposite is also true. If your actions are
negative, guess what your thoughts are gonna be? You don't
believe me? Well, here's a little test you can do to prove it to
yourself. Lie in a dark room on the couch for several hours
without movin'. Just lie there and watch TV. Don't get up for
nothin', except maybe to get some junk food out of the kitchen.
When you finally do get your butt up off that couch, what do
you think your first thoughts are gonna be? How do you think
you're gonna feel?

I guarantee you won't feel like a winner. You'll probably feel
tired, worn out, and grouchy. Your energy level will be lower
than usual. Some of you might even feel like you're in the early
stages of gettin' sick.

Or think about how you felt the last time you came off the court
after playin' some good B-ball with your buddies. No matter
how depressed you might be goin' into the game, if you play
basketball for a couple hours, you're gonna walk off the court
feelin' pumped, and a lot better than you did when you walked
onto the court — even if you lost. That's because your body
wasn't created to lie in a dark room in front of a TV. Your body
was built for movement and action.

Changin' People, Places, And Things
Have you ever noticed that in school the bullies hang together,
the straight A students hang together, and the jocks and cheer-
leaders all hang together? If you're in a gang or a pot smokin',
gettin' high, or drinkin' crowd, you may want to take a long
look at where you're headed.

Gettin' through the between time has to include changin' the people you hang with, the places you hang out, and the way you spend your time. It's real important to surround yourself with people who are really in your corner — people who are part of the solution and not the old problem.

Let's face it, like attracts like. If all you do is hang out with the same old people, and talk about the same old stuff, guess what's gonna be next. It's gonna be the same-old, same-old every time. Before you know it, you're gonna be right back doin' the same old junk.

My second wife, Terri helped me see this. We were startin' a new business and a new life together, and we figured that we'd have a better chance at succeedin' if we were able to focus all of our energy on movin' forward, instead of havin' to deal with the distractions of the past. So we sold our house and, in the middle of winter, moved to a little place in northern Minnesota called Moose Lake.

Now, I don't know if any of you have ever heard of Moose Lake, but let me tell you, livin' up there is like bein' somewhere between Nowhere and Siberia. That winter it was so cold, I didn't have *time* to think about anything but stayin' warm and how much I hated bein' there. And believe me, I thought a lot about that!

I'm not tellin' you that you have to move to Siberia in order to make it through the between time — but you might just have to move across town. The important thing is for you to be willin' to do whatever it takes, or go wherever you have to in order to improve your chances at havin' a new life.

A friend of mine told me that not only did she have to move away from where she had been livin', she had to stop goin' to certain types of places, and stop listenin' to certain music for a while. She told me that she always used to listen to blues singers like Billy Holiday and Nina Simone when she was gettin' high. She loved the blues, and these ladies were her favorite singers, but she gave away all of her albums because when she'd listen to them, she automatically started cravin' drugs.

The songs she used to listen to became triggers for negative thinkin' and actions. So she gave 'em up. You might not have to get that drastic, but check yourself out. Each of us has our own list of things that make us want to go back to our old lives. Find out what yours are, and then keep away from them.

Think About It

- *Spiritual beliefs give life meaning. They focus on the big picture instead of just the drama of the moment.*
- *Everything you do, good and bad, comes back to you. What you put out is what you get back.*
- *Why is it we figure the unknown is always gonna be worse than what we're doin' now? Why don't we automatically believe that it's filled with exciting possibilities that are just waitin' for us to take the first steps?*

CHAPTER 26

Attitudes and Beliefs
That Will Keep You Stuck

Fear Of Success

That's right — I said fear of success. You'd probably be surprised at how many people actually fear success more than they do failure. So they become spectators.

Spectators are the great fearful silent majority. They'd much rather sit on their butts and watch life happen to other people than risk the possibility of success. They're channel-surfin' couch potatoes whose idea of bein' in control means holdin' the remote! They're comfortable with failure 'cuz they know what that's like. They're afraid of takin' a risk, so they want to keep you stuck. They'll be the first to laugh at your new ideas, and the first to tell you "I told you so" when you experience setbacks.

Take a look at your own life. Have you given yourself permission to be successful? No, I'm not jokin'. This may sound like a silly question to you, but it's an important one to ask yourself. You're the one who has to make that choice; nobody can make it for you. And you know what? You don't have to wait until you're an adult to decide.

As a kid, I was afraid that my friends wouldn't like me anymore if I was successful. This was one of the things that kept me stuck. I also believed that some of my friends really didn't want me to succeed because they were afraid I'd leave them behind. Guess what! If you've ever felt like this, you just might need new friends.

Victim Thinking

People limit themselves by believin' that they're never good enough. They're professional victims who constantly put themselves down. They think the grass is always greener somewhere else. They whine, they complain. They believe that success is somethin' that's given to special people at birth. Many of them waste their whole lives envyin' and criticizin' others.

They think everyone else has it made, or at the very least has it a lot better than them. They resent the success of others, and blame circumstances and other people for the misery in their lives.

Well, buddy, you know what? Believin' you're a victim keeps you stuck. We hear a lot of talk today about victims: victims of poverty, victims of prejudice, victims of circumstances, victims of abuse, victim's rights. Well, I'm here to tell you that no matter who you are, where you live, or what you've experienced, you can choose *not* to be a victim.

When I was a kid, I used to look at the lives of other people — especially popular athletes, musicians, and other celebrities — and think, "Man, I hate my life! I wish I was them — I'd have it made. They're soooo lucky. Everybody respects them." I believed that people who had power, popularity, and success were carefree and always happy. I couldn't imagine that they ever felt lonely, or unloved, or worthless. I believed that I was the only one who ever felt like that.

Who can get caught in the victim trap? Are you kiddin'? We all can. Every one of us. I've never met anyone who hasn't been caught in this trap at some point in their lives. Everyone goes through hard times once in a while. The point is, you don't have to live there.

Popularity, wealth, and fame don't keep people from fallin' into the trap. Just look at the number of successful athletes, musicians, and celebrities who get caught. The gossip magazines are filled with stories about famous people whose lives and careers have been cut short because they can't cope with success.

Here are a couple of ways you can trick yourself into a lifetime of bein' a victim. The first way is for you to believe that *you're not responsible for what you do* — that everyone else is to blame. For instance,

- You lie because your mom has to work and doesn't greet you at the door every day you come home from school with home-baked cookies and milk.
- You steal because some basketball player got paid big bucks to tell you that you're nothin' if you don't wear the shoes he's hypin'.
- You get high because your mom's a witch who yells all the time, and never lets you do anything you want.
- You beat your girlfriend because your old man beats you and your mom.
- You shot that dude because he ticked you off and MTV and Hollywood told you that you're a punk if you let it slide.

Another way you can put yourself in the victim trickbag is by always believin' that *you* are to blame for everything. You buy into everybody else's b.s., and accept guilt and blame for whatever they want to lay on you. For example,

- If you didn't make him so mad, he wouldn't beat you up.
- If you were whiter, blacker, taller, shorter, bigger, skinnier, better lookin' — the list goes on and on and on — you'd be treated better.
- If you looked different or acted differently you wouldn't have been raped.
- You think "Poor me. I'm worthless and no good. I might as well die."

If you believe any of these statements, then you're on your way to bein' a victim.   But it's not too late to avoid the trap.

What happens when people blame you for things that really aren't your responsibility?   Do you get mad and blame them back?   Or do you get depressed and feel bad about yourself? Either way, you've just given up your personal power and gotten yourself stuck in the victim trap.

I Can't vs. I Won't

Let's get honest with this one.   'Cuz when we say "I can't," we're usually really sayin', "I don't want to."   And you know what?   That's OK.   If you're not ready or you don't want to, that's your choice.   Just be honest about it.   At least then you've got the option to change your mind.   But when you tell yourself and others "I can't" — where you gonna go from there?   Nowhere!   You stay stuck in "I can't."

Anger

First of all, anger isn't good or bad.   It's just a powerful physical and emotional response.   Anger's never our first feelin' — it protects us from the pain of things like fear, frustration, hurt, humiliation, embarrassment, helplessness, rejection, and sadness.   It's usually safer for us to be angry than to feel any of these other emotions.

Just like fire, if anger's controlled it can be a positive thing.   But once it's out of control, it can destroy everything in its path.

Look, I'm not sayin' that you don't have the right to ever get angry. Of course you do. If someone who knows what you're about deliberately hurts you or treats you unfairly, then you have a right to feel angry!

If you know how to use it, anger can give you extra energy for tough jobs. It can inspire you to work harder to get what you want. The feelin' of anger is an important sign that lets you know when something's wrong and you need to deal with it.

Usin' anger in a healthy way — not gettin' violent or out of control, not ranting or raving — can help you communicate negative feelings, relieve tension, and even resolve conflicts. Anger can actually help tear down barriers which keep people apart. That's if it's used in the right way.

When you begin to control your anger, you can learn to use its energy to make positive changes in your life or your community.

The thing is, you'll either control your anger or it'll control you. Uncontrolled anger makes you say or do things you'll deeply regret later. It can lead to revenge and violence.

Have you ever noticed that when you're with someone who's out of control, you hardly ever hear what they're saying? Instead, all you want to do is protect yourself by shuttin' down, numbin' out, and gettin' angry, or gettin' as far away from them as you can.

There are a lot of things you can do to interrupt the anger pattern and gain control of it. One is to simply get out of the situation for a little while. Take a short time-out and then come back to deal with the issue. But remember, if you don't return to deal with the situation, the anger will only continue to build and the problem will get worse.

Leavin' the situation gives your body time to cool off, and your emotions a chance to calm down. Takin' a walk, joggin', cleanin' the garage, or punchin' a bag will help discharge some of the extra energy and tension in your body. Once you've been able to calm down and cool off, you'll be able to think more clearly about the situation and it'll be easier to solve.

If you're in a situation where it's not possible for you to leave for a while, here are some things to try that have helped me and other people:

- If you're in a car, try listenin' to three songs on the radio. Or stop and get gas, or walk around your car.
- If you're at school or at work, take a ten-minute bath room break, or go and get a drink of water. Put your hands in some cool water or put a cool paper towel on the back of your neck. You can also try deep breathin', countin' to fifty, changin' your physical position, or smilin'.
- Think of somethin' funny. How long do you think you can stay angry if you're laughin'?

The World Doesn't Owe You a Thing

Nowadays, for some reason, we've gotten the idea that we're entitled to everything we see advertised on television.
Anything anybody else has, we feel we should have, too.

This b.s. feelin' of entitlement leads to killin' the kid down the street 'cuz he's wearin' a certain coat or a pair of overpriced shoes. Some crazy wannabe sees 'em and thinks the only way to be cool is to be seen wearin' em — so he takes the kid's life, and then he takes his shoes. You know I'm not lyin'. Now, what's up with that? Am I supposed to believe that you think a pair of shoes or a coat is worth more than life?

How many people think they deserve a high-payin' job — or

welfare? It's just too easy to start thinkin' that we deserve everything we want — and then to get violent when we don't get it.

Now, listen up. You know that's actin' like a two-year-old who wants his mommy to buy him a lollypop, and then throws a fit in the middle of the store if he doesn't get it. Only here are guys 15, 25, 35, and 40 years old, thinkin' everybody owes 'em whatever they want. Man, it's time to grow up and learn to take "no" for an answer without thinkin' or actin' like it's the end of the whole world.

Think About It

- *Spectators are the great fearful silent majority. They'd much rather sit and watch life happen to other people than risk the possibility of success.*
- *Victims limit themselves by believin' that they're never good enough.*
- *You can choose NOT to be a victim.*
- *When you tell yourself and others, "I can't"— where you gonna go from there? Nowhere! You stay stuck in "I can't."*

CHAPTER 27

Hang Tough —
Keep On
Keepin' On

Stayin' In The Present Moment

How many people do you know who go through their whole lives worryin' about what might happen? I've been there and done that, so I know how easy this is to fall into. You know, there's a fine line between plannin' for tomorrow and worryin' about tomorrow. In fact, a lot of people think they're plannin' when all they're really doin' is worryin'.

Or what about the blame game we play with ourselves when we make a mistake? It's helpful to figure out what you've done wrong so you can learn from your mistakes. But it's totally bogus — and does you no good — to start hatin' yourself 'cuz you didn't do something perfectly.

The great thing about learnin' to stay in the present moment is that all the bad things that happened yesterday — or last year — don't exist in the here and now. Each day is a new day, with new possibilities and opportunities.

Now it's up to you. You can waste your precious time and energy belly-achin' about what went on in the past, or worryin' about what might happen tomorrow. But you can't do anything about the past, and the only thing you can do about the future is to make sure that today you're doin' the things which will increase your chances of *havin'* a future .

How To Get a Rush Without a Risk

One of the things about life out on the street is the rush we get from playin' the game. We fool ourselves into thinkin' the only way to experience the rush is to be out there hustlin' and playin' or gettin' high.

We get hooked on the drama of the game, and pretty soon that rush is the only way we have of tellin' that we're still alive.

But if it's the rush you're after, what about bungee jumpin' or sky divin'? Parachuting out of an airplane at 30,000 feet is a bigger — and safer — rush than walkin' down an alley, lookin' up, and realizin' that you're surrounded by 30 gang members, and none of them are wearin' your colors.

Bungee jumpin's got to be a lot bigger rush than jumpin' from garage to garage or roof to roof to get away from the cops. And I guarantee that scuba divin' is a lot more fun than jumpin' into a dirty river hopin' the cops don't see ya. Or what about trainin' to be a member of the bomb squad or SWAT team or Navy Seals? These guys get paid for their adrenaline rushes. Do ya think you could hang with the big boys?

One of the hardest things I had to fight when I left the life was boredom. I didn't know what to do with myself. For ten years I'd been livin' in the fast lane — existin' on adrenaline and cocaine. What was I supposed to do now? There was a huge hole left in my life, and I had to fill it up with somethin' positive, or you can guess where I would've ended up.

I handled it first by becomin' addicted to runnin'. Then I found out that the rush I got from givin' instead of takin', volunteering and helpin' other people, was better than any high I'd experienced before.

I got back ten times more than I ever gave. I began to look for new ways to help me keep that feelin' of well-being everybody's lookin' for. But this time I knew that only a temporary, false sense of well-being comes from the end of a needle. I wanted more than that.

What To Do When You Blow It

Makin' mistakes and havin' failures is all part of the learnin' process. The important thing is to learn from it. Remember, every mistake you make today can be one less you're gonna make tomorrow — if you choose to learn from your mistakes instead of gettin' stuck in 'em. Everybody blows it sometime. Be patient with yourself! Don't worry about what other people think or say.

So you fell on your face, just like so and so said you would. Does that make you a failure? No! You don't have nothin' to be ashamed of, so don't fall into the old blame and shame game. Life ain't about blame and shame, it's about listenin' and learnin'. Mistakes are lessons — we just have to have the courage to go through 'em, learn from 'em, and go on.

Look, the sun don't come up new every 24 hours for nothin'. It's the Creator's way of tellin' us we've been given another chance. So, brother, take that chance, and get on with it.

When All Else Fails, Fake It 'Til You Make It

In other words, don't give up just because you don't *feel* like hangin' in there. Remember your plan and stick with it, whether you feel like it or not. Feelings are wonderful, but we don't have to be slaves to them. There's an old saying in Colorado, "If you don't like our weather, stick around until this afternoon."

Well, let me tell you, feelings can change just as quickly as Colorado weather.

So you're havin' a bad day, or a bad week? Well, nothin' lasts forever, and that includes bad days. There've been plenty of times I didn't feel like workin' out, but I hauled my butt to the gym and did it anyway. By the time I was finished workin' out, I'd forgotten all about why I hadn't wanted to be there in the first place.

If you're havin' a bad day and all else fails, then fake it. Start smilin'. If someone asks you how you're doin', say great! Say hi to everyone you meet. Focus on other people instead of yourself, and after a while you'll notice you really *do* start feelin' better. It's all about your attitude.

Look, success doesn't depend on perfection or speed, it only depends on the direction your attitude is takin' you.

Think About It

- *Stay in the present moment.*
- *If a rush is what you're after, try bungee jumpin' or sky divin'. It's a whole lot safer than life on the street.*
- *Success depends on the direction your attitude is takin' you.*

CHAPTER 28

What Most "Feel Good" Experts Won't Tell You About Success

The Rest Of The Story

It's been thirteen years since I decided to get off the street, and I've never been happier about my life. I make a decent living doing what I love. I eat well and exercise. My spiritual life is my highest priority. I have loyal friends who love me and who are as close to me as family. I have a great relationship with my three boys. They are my heart, and my favorite companions.

And if this were a fairy tale, that would be the whole story and I'd end it by saying, "And he lived happily ever after. THE END."

Only this ain't no fairy tale! "Happily ever after" ain't for real. It's fiction created to sell books and movies. In life, there's no such thing as a perfect ending.

Our real lives are filled with good times, bad times, happiness, sadness, success, and failure. All of us are walkin' forward, and sometimes stumblin', as we deal with the challenges we're faced with.

That's right, I said stumblin'. In fact, some days, just like you, it seems I spend more time dustin' off my backside than I do on my feet.

Why am I tellin' you this? 'Cuz I want you to know more than just the facts about how to turn your life around — I want you to know the truth.

It's easy to blow off people who talk and write about success if you think that they've had it better than you, or they're stronger, smarter, or luckier than you. Don't even try to go there with me! I'm no different than you, and if I can turn my life around, you can.

I'm Not Perfect — Nobody Is

The fact that I had the guts to sit down with a couple of my friends and write about my life — the good, the bad, and the criminal — doesn't make me a hero.

The fact that I used to flip a lot of dope, and survived to tell about it, doesn't make me an expert on life. I'm just somebody who found my way off the streets, and I've shared it with you in hopes that you might have the guts to try it, so hopefully you won't make the destructive decisions that I did.

If It Were So Easy, Everybody'd Be Doin' It!

I've already told you what it was like for me during the between time, that no-man's-land between the street life and the straight life. It was scary and it was hard.

But now that I've been more or less straight for thirteen years, I don't have to struggle anymore. I'm free of self-doubt, I always speak from my heart, my business is booming, and it pretty much runs itself. Basically, I've reached the point in my life at age 45 where life is a breeze: no doubts, no struggle, no pain...

And if you buy that, I have some beach-front property in the desert I want to sell you!

The truth is, my life is no different than anybody else's. I still struggle with fear and self-doubt, only now I don't let them completely control me. If it were easy, everybody'd be livin' a balanced life filled with happiness and success.

I Still Struggle With Fear And Doubt

Take this book, for example. It exists even though I've had fears that I wasn't good enough to write it. I mean, really, who am I to think that I could write a book that would effect anybody's life? How did I know that anybody would even read it, let alone take a chance at applying the things I've shared? After all, I'm not a professional athlete, or a rock or rap star, or some other celebrity. I'm just a regular guy, an ex-street punk who knew there had to be more to life than the b.s. I was involved in, and by grace had the courage to go find out what it was.

It hasn't been easy. Yeah, I got discouraged, and at times I wondered what I was doin' — but I didn't quit. It's taken me through the process of hurt and pain, success and failure. But I didn't give up, I grew with it.

How Do Ya Know
When To Trust Your Feelings?

It took me a while, but I finally learned that the only time I can really count on my feelings to reflect the truth is when they come from my heart. The rest of the time, they're not good or bad, they're just feelings.

When I was young, I was afraid of my feelings and ashamed of my fears. Today I'm not afraid of my feelings, and I'm not ashamed of my fears. I don't have to be tough all the time. I've learned to experience the power that comes from speaking the truth about whatever I'm feelin'. And most of the time, I control my feelings, instead of them controlling me.

Learnin' To Control Yourself
Is a Lifelong Process

Do I always say the right thing? No. Do I always handle my feelings in the best way? Heck, no! Like everyone, I'm still in process. My anger still gets the best of me at times, and I end up payin' for it in more ways than I like to think about.

Like the time 13 years ago, when I went to a friend's house with some of my buddies to watch a Green Bay Packers game. Before the game I had called my bookie in Milwaukee and put $500 on a seven-point spread. I'd also made a few small side bets with some of my friends. At the end of the first half, the score was 20-0, and I had begun to loudly tell the guys they'd better get their money out.

By the end of the third quarter, I was dancin' in the streets and doin' cartwheels because my team was still winnin'. I was loudly celebratin' where I was gonna take my old lady to dinner that night, and how I was gonna spend the rest of my $500.

With only seven minutes left in the game, I was ready to collect my money and leave. Thinkin' that this was the easiest money I'd ever made, I began wishin' that I had bet $10,000 instead of $500.

By now, you've probably guessed how the story ends. I've never seen a team make a turn-around so fast in my life. In just six minutes and 59 seconds, the other team made three touchdowns, and the guys began to really rub my face in it. The score at the end of the game was 24-21. Green Bay won by three points, not seven. How happy do you think I was then? They won the game, but I lost my bet! And in six minutes and 59 seconds, I went from bein' a happy-go-lucky, rich Dr. Jekyll to a violent, demon-possessed loser, Mr. Hyde. I got so mad at the thought of losin' that I actually picked up my friend's TV and tossed it through a plate glass window in his house.

That day, my lack of control cost me my pride and $1700: $500 on the game and $1200 to replace the window and TV set.

Weeks later I still felt like the biggest jerk in the world because I'd let myself lose it over a stupid bet, and as a result had almost lost a good friend in the process. After it was all over, I realized that I didn't even have a good time watchin' the game because I was so stressed out about whether or not I was goin' to win the bet.

And then it dawned on me that this was not the only time I had been miserable and gotten out of control when I bet on professional sports. It was a pattern for me — one I decided that I could live without. And so I quit gamblin'.

Since that time, I've learned better ways to deal with anger. But I'd be lyin' if I let you think that my anger never gets the best of me anymore. It's one of the areas of my life I'm still workin' on.

Nobody Believes In Themselves *All* The Time

I used to think that successful people believed in themselves all the time: that they always had it together, no matter what. But guess what? That's *crazy!* Everybody has an off day sometimes. In fact, most successful people wrestle with fear and self-doubt their whole lives.

There are days I still get caught up in my old negative attitude, but I don't stay stuck in it. My spiritual beliefs help get me out of the old self-destructive doubts and fears.

I've learned that there are no mistakes in life. I believe everything that happens is God's will and for the highest good. In fact, I have a sign hangin' in my office that says, *"If you knew who walked beside you on the way that you have chosen, fear would be impossible."*

The More You Give, The More You Get

Early in my life I believed that I was entitled to whatever I thought I wanted at the time. I wanted *what* I wanted, *when* I wanted it, and I always found a way to get it. I was a taker.

At home and at school, I believed that I shouldn't have to do anything I didn't want to do. In fact, I worked real hard at *not* doin' what I didn't feel like doin'. I bribed and manipulated my way through high school. I never did my best at anything, except my schemes to get out of work. I went out of my way not to do what was expected of me.

The six years I was in the Army I worked harder at not doin' what I was told than the GI Joes ever do to win promotions. If there was a job that should have taken 15 minutes to do, I'd take 45 minutes to get out of doin' it. As a result, I was transferred more times than the Army would like to admit. It's a miracle I didn't spend all six years in the brig.

When I went to work at the brewery, I spent all my time figurin' out how to do as little as I possibly could. My motto, was "I'll do it my way," and my way was whichever way the company *didn't* want it done.

It wasn't until I went into the dope business and began to hire my own employees that I began to understand the laws that govern givin' and receivin'. Loyalty and dependability became very important to me when I was flippin' dope. I learned that the best way to insure that my people would be loyal to me was for me to be totally loyal to them. In fact, the more loyal they were to me, the more I gave back to them.

After I started workin' in the straight world, I began to realize that a lot of people were like I had been as a kid. Most people are only willin' to give just enough to get by. They give what the average guy gives, and as a result, they end up livin' the boring life that the average guy lives. They've never learned to go for the gold, to give 100%. Instead, they'd rather live their lives envyin' those who do.

Bein' self-employed has taught me that I will only get back what I put out, and that the more I give out, the more I get back in return.

Fallin' Down Isn't Failure Unless You're Too Lazy To Get Up

I started gettin' high when I was a kid. In my house, it was acceptable for us kids to drink, and it was no big deal if we got drunk. I got high almost every day for more than 20 years. I'd be lyin' if I told you that I never feel like gettin' high anymore.

The truth is, in the past 13 years there've been times that I drank more than I should have. But I didn't use this as an excuse to throw my life away. I picked myself up, and started all over again.

Things Don't Always Go Right The First Time

My point is, you're not gonna get it right the first time around. You're gonna have times when you fall back into old patterns of thinkin' and actin'. That's okay — in fact, it's normal. Just don't get stuck in the drama. Get up, hose yourself down, and keep on keepin' on. Fallin' down is not a failure unless you're too lazy to get up! In fact, the more times you fall flat on your face and pick yourself up, the better your chances are at succeedin'.

Temptation Is Always Lookin' To Find You

I handled lots of money during the ten years I sold dope. I was good at it...easy come, easy go. In the beginning I told myself that I'd get out after I made $100,000. But there was always the thought of that one last big score. Eventually I got sick of the game, and I wanted a better life. I hated the dyin' and death that were all around me.

But you know what? Gettin' out of the business was as much of a process as gettin' in. I didn't just quit and walk away one day. It took me about twelve months to get myself physically out of the business. I'd quit mentally, emotionally, and spiritually a long time before I actually made my last sale.

Be patient with yourself. You didn't get into this mess overnight. You're not gonna get out overnight. Give yourself time to grow into your new life. Keep walkin' in the right direction, and eventually you'll end up there.

What Goes Around, Comes Around
Just between you and me, there've been times over the past 13 years when I was tempted to go for that final big score. I even came up with some very justifiable reasons why I needed the money. But I never did fall for this sucker trap because of one thing: karma, the law of cause and effect. I've learned that what goes around, comes around. Every one of us reaps exactly what we sow.

Dope money is dirty money. No matter what you do with it, it's still dirty. You may not spend a day in the joint, but somewhere down the line you'll have to pay for havin' it. Maybe not today, or tomorrow, but sometime during this lifetime it will come back on you. This is what's kept me out of the drug business. I don't want to keep payin' the consequences.

Nowadays I'm conscious of the principles of the law of karma. I've figured out that what I give out, I get back. There's just no way around it. This helps me be smarter about the decisions I make in my life, and I'm a lot more careful now about where I invest my time and energy.

Life Rocks. Life Sucks.
Both Are True All The Time
Just hear me out before you decide all that coke fried one too

many brain cells and that I'm out of my mind. The truth is, at any time in your life, no matter what's happenin', you can find somethin' to be happy about, and you can find somethin' to complain about.

When we're young we always think that money and fame will bring us happiness. But let's look at the facts. A lot of times people who look good on paper are more miserable than you.

Some Great Wisdom From Biggie Smalls

Take Biggie Smalls, for example. When he first started out he was motivated by money and the love of the game. He did his thing, people responded, and he was out in front with money, women, and fame. So he must have been happy. He must have had it all together, right?

Wrong! Just before he was killed, he admitted that he had lost his love of the game and that he was only hangin' in for the money. He was all tied up with controversies, rumor, jealousies, and accusations.

> "...I swear it's a headache... I've really been talkin'
> about quittin'. I really want to stop. If I was finan-
> cially stable I would... I would quit... I just wanna
> be in a calm area... I just wanna relax."
>   Biggie Smalls

The best of times, the worst of times. He'd never had it so good in all his life. He'd never had it so bad, either.

Or look at Michael Jackson. He's one of the richest entertainers in the world, and definitely one of the most famous. Yet the man can't walk down the street in peace. He has every material thing he could ever want, but he also lives a life filled with disappointment, isolation, and pain.

This isn't true just for people who are rich and famous. It's the same for all of us. There is good and bad in everyone's life. *No one* lives a pain-free life.

A Lot Of Good Can Come Out Of Pain

Mother's Against Drunk Drivers (MADD) has been credited with changin' the whole country's attitude about drunk drivin'. The woman who started this movement is a mother whose teenage daughter was killed by a drunk driver. As a result of her efforts, the lives of thousands of people are saved every year.

Every situation in our lives has the potential to bring something good and something bad into our lives. *We* are the ones who have the power to decide which it will be. Whatever we choose to focus on will increase in our lives.

You Are Alive Right Now For a Special Reason

Find that reason. Embrace it, celebrate it! It's your purpose for livin'. Each one of us has something special that makes us feel good when we do it. What's your talent, your special skill? If you know what it is, then go do it. Have fun. If you don't know, then take the time out to find what it is. Do what you love and the money will follow. But don't take my word for it. Go find the truth of this for yourself.

And lighten up! Laugh at yourself and your circumstances for a change. Be in the moment, and have fun with whatever you're doin'. In fact, laugh every chance you get. It's good for your body, mind, and soul.

Now It's Your Turn —

So Go For It!

About Allen Fahden

Allen Fahden is an international author, speaker, strategic consultant, and corporate trainer on innovation and creativity. In the publicity for his first book, *Innovation On Demand* (The Illiterati, 1992, 281 pg.), he has appeared in People Magazine, ABC News, BBC TV, countless television and radio broadcasts, as well as syndicated and local print media across the US.

The Innovate with C.A.R.E. profile system, identifying people as Creators, Advancers, Refiners, or Executors, and the work processes associated with it, have been implemented in businesses in the US as well as, Japan, Germany, England, South Africa, Malaysia, and Australia.

Organizations that have adopted Mr. Fahden's book, seminars and techniques include: GE-Capital, Coca-Cola, Nissan, U.S. West, 3M, DuPont, Saturn, Cargill, Eastman-Kodak, Volvo, Ceridian, Deloitte Touche, United Health, and Saturn.

About Judy Grant

Judy Grant is a writer, speaker, and psychiatric nurse who, over the past 28 years, has worked extensively with at-risk children and criminal adults.

She was part of a team which developed poly-substance abuse programs for kids, as well as the first federally funded methadone treatment clinics in the Midwest. She has worked as an addictions counselor, facilitated therapy groups for addicted prisoners within the federal prison system, and support groups for women.

Ms. Grant currently resides in Colorado, and is in the process of developing curriculum for adolescent girls.

Meet
Ron Glodoski

Ron speaks from the heart of real life experience. He has lived — and thrived — on both sides of the law. He's a dynamic business-man who survived an abusive childhood by escaping to the street.

At age 12, he was a gang member. By the time he was 15, he was a gang leader with a felony record consisting of armed robbery, strong-armed robbery, assault and battery, and car theft. In his twen-ties, he became one of the most successful drug dealers in Milwau-kee — commanding an extensive criminal network.

He built this extremely successful criminal business by develop-ing and following a series of rules for success — rules which, he discovered later, also apply to most straight businesses.

After 20 years as a criminal, Ron hit rock bottom and finally woke up. He had lost his family, and most of his friends were either dead or doing time. He wanted out of the gangster life.

His decision to change his life led him on a path to self-discov-ery. He stopped dealing and using drugs, and began successfully applying his skills to a series of legitimate businesses — including a teddy bear company he grew from a home-based business to a company employing 35 people and generating $1.8 million a year.

Today he is an author and motivational speaker; leads work-shops and support groups on gang life, violence prevention, and drug and alcohol abuse; is a volunteer counselor for social service agencies; and a popular speaker in schools, prisons, and detention centers.

As someone who has been there and made it through, Ron reaches out to kids with respect, and teaches them how to take back their right to choose a better way of life. He shows them how to use street smarts to improve themselves and escape their personal hell.

"Students see through the bull very quickly, so to hold them the whole time is a testament to his story and its worth to young and old. Thank God he has come forward to tell his story."

> Terrance L. Andrew
> Teacher/Therapist
> Menlo Park Alternative High School

"Honest, passionate, warm, straightforward and powerful. These are the words that explain Ron Glodoski's presentation to our class. Students are facing an everyday battle with drugs, crime and violence. Many of them believe that they are trapped in that lifestyle forever and the only way to convince them that things can change is to show them. Ron is one who can show students that it is possible to climb out of the trenches. When students see someone who has been at the bottom and made it to the top, they start to listen and believe in themselves."

> Scott Kowalski
> Teacher/Coach
> Expo Middle School

"Ron's message held the students' attention because he was identified by them as knowing what he is talking about. His message...was delivered forcefully and clearly. The fact that he talks from personal experience gives credence to his message."

> Tom Russ
> Supervisor
> Ramsey County Community Corrections Department

The Program

The Real Deal
On Crime, Drugs, and Easy Money

Helps Kids Avoid:
- *destructive decisions*
- *the powerful seduction of gang life*
- *drug and alcohol abuse*
- *violence and peer pressure*

Ron's no-nonsense, hard-hitting message captivates his audiences. They listen in awe to someone who's done what most of them have only seen in movies.

Having experienced the darkest side of gangs, crime, drugs, and violence, Ron strips away the mystery of the gangster life and reveals the suffering and terror that stalk those who live outside the law.

He goes beyond the illusion of the tough front and the cool image. He reaches kids who feel alienated by the system and are on the brink of making choices that could destroy the rest of their lives.

For more information about booking Ron for your school, group, or organization, call or write:

Turn Around Publishing
P.O. Box 803
Pewaukee, WI 53072-0803

Toll-free: 1-800-968-6863
E-mail: tapteam@att.net

**For more information about books, tapes, and seminars by Ron Glodoski,
Contact:**

Turn Around Publishing
P.O. Box 803
Pewaukee, WI 53072-0803

Toll-free:
1-800-968-6863

E-mail:
tapteam@att.net